When I Think of Bobby

When I Think of Bobby

A PERSONAL MEMOIR
OF THE KENNEDY YEARS

Warren Rogers

HarperPerennial
A Division of HarperCollinsPublishers

A hardcover edition of this book was published in 1993 by HarperCollins Publishers.

HarperCollins books may be purchased for educational, business, or sales promotional use. For information please write: Special Markets Department, HarperCollins Publishers, Inc., 10 East 53rd Street, New York, NY 10022.

First HarperPerennial edition published 1994.

Designed by George J. McKeon

The Library of Congress has catalogued the hardcover edition as follows:

Rogers, Warren.
    When I think of Bobby : a personal memoir of the Kennedy years / by Warren Rogers.—1st ed.
      p. cm.
    Includes index.
    ISBN 0-06-017042-5
    1. Kennedy, Robert F., 1925–1968—Friends and associates. 2. Rogers, Warren. 3. Kennedy family. 4. Legislators—United States—Biography. 5. Cabinet officers—United States—Biography. 6. Presidential candidates—United States—Biography. 7. United States. Congress. Senate—Biography. I. Title.
E840.8.K4R586 1993
973.922'092—dc20   92-56244

ISBN 0-06-092533-7 (pbk.)

94 95 96 97 98 ❖/RRD 10 9 8 7 6 5 4 3 2 1

For Ena Bernard, who came to Hickory Hill as an employee and stayed as family. She reminisced about it all much later. Perhaps missing the innocence of the times, when everybody was much younger and things were less complicated, Ena sighed, "Those were fun days."

Contents

A section of illustrations follows page 114.

Preface

When I Think of Bobby is a love story. It is the story of the love that Robert and Ethel Kennedy shared at the home they created at Hickory Hill, for each other, for their children and for all who knew them. This book is not about Marilyn Monroe. It is not about Frank Sinatra or his relations with the Kennedys, or Chappaquiddick, or Palm Beach, or even Camelots that used to be or Camelots that never were. It is not about Jack Kennedy or Ted Kennedy or the father, Joseph P. Kennedy, or their peccadillos and foibles, if any, which, after all, were theirs and not Robert Kennedy's. It is not in the spirit of what today passes for journalism, the hearsay and gossip presented as fact and even then sensationalized. It is none of that.

When I Think of Bobby seeks to capture the essence of the character, curiosity, wit, honesty and love of family that propelled a remarkable man who inspired millions and whose impact is still being felt today. It is told in narrative and anecdote by one who knew him and went out with him "to seek a newer world," in the phrase he borrowed from Alfred Tennyson, and through interviews with Ethel Kennedy, her children and friends and family retainers. The Kennedy family agreed to cooperate with the author, and it has done so through good times and bad.

The inspiration for the book comes from something Robert Kennedy once said to the author, who was then *LOOK* magazine's Washington editor, as he broke off an interview: "I've got to go. Excuse me. I don't want to be rude, but I've got to go. My children are waiting for me to play with them. I promised."

What of those children to whom he gave such priority and such promises? How well did his special nurturing succeed? How did they turn out? Well, one, to whom he seemed to pay particular attention, died of a drug overdose in his early twenties. Another fought a battle with drugs, apparently won and became an environmental lawyer and activist. The eldest, wife of a college professor and raising their children, ran for Congress, lost and planned to run again. The second born won a seat in the U.S. Congress from Massachusetts, and a younger brother quit a prestigious law firm to take over from him the nonprofit group he founded in Boston that supplies home fuel oil to the poor at reduced prices. They and all their sisters and brothers, down to the youngest of the eleven, work with their mother on the various foundations that are their father's legacy. The list is impressively long, and the Robert Kennedy theme of humanity and compassion prevails through them all: foundations to fight against cancer and child neglect and aid the mentally retarded, for instance, and to promote excellence in journalism and books about helping the disadvantaged, to encourage art by the handicapped, and to honor the champions of human rights worldwide. Through the confused seventies and the permissive eighties, Bob and Ethel's children turned out all right.

Shortly after midnight on June 5, 1968, Robert Kennedy lay dying of an assassin's bullet on the floor of the kitchen of the Ambassador Hotel in Los Angeles, California. The author was there, with Ethel, helping her tend her fallen husband. With two campaign aides, Frederick G. Dutton and William G. Barry, they rushed Robert Kennedy to a hospital. But he died, and an era died with him.

The world had seen him as a brilliant manager of his brother John's campaigns for the House and Senate and White House, as U.S. Attorney General, as U.S. Senator from New York, and as a different kind of candidate for the presidency himself. Nobody can say with certainty what sort of President he might have been. Yet, we do know there would have been no continuation of the Vietnam debacle because he would have ended the war in March of 1969, as he pledged, saving thirty-five thousand Americans from death, and no Watergate scandal because he and not Richard M. Nixon would have been in the White House in 1972, and there would have been much, much more progress on civil rights and tolerance of racial diversity in America. Surely, we would be living in a different and perhaps a better world.

That was the public Robert Kennedy, who came to politics because it was fun and stayed because it was a duty and a responsibility and a chance to do good. Millions of words have been written about him. *When I Think of Bobby* goes beyond that and focuses on the private Robert Kennedy, husband and father, uncle and surrogate father to the children of his assassinated brother John, off guard with friends, troubled at times but often at ease and playful, the squire of historic Hickory Hill, which had been the Civil War headquarters of General George Brinton McClellan and later the home of Supreme Court Justice Robert H. Jackson. Robert and Ethel made Hickory Hill the center of their own private world. The real Robert Kennedy came alive there. The real Ethel too.

This is an affectionate portrait of Robert F. Kennedy a quarter-century after his death, told by those who knew him best. The narrative touches on his public life, but the focus is on his private life, away from the spotlight, among family and friends, at Hickory Hill and elsewhere, and on his extraordinary capacity, throughout his life, for personal growth. The essence is anecdotes that draw the picture, not a eulogy, but a warm portrait of a loving, loyal, tough, idealistic man. It is useless to seek the "ruthless Robert" of crime-fighting and politics at Hickory Hill, although there is relentlessness in his pursuit of excellence in himself and those he loved, even at play and around the dinner table. And there is no trace of the philanderer invented by the new wave of Kennedy-bashers who would visit the sins of the brothers as well as the father on him. Such a Bob Kennedy there never was.

This book is for those whose idealism was mobilized by Robert Kennedy, and who worked for his causes, and for others whose hopes for a better world survive even the loss that will always be "unacceptable," in one of his words. It is also for those, too young to have been personally aware of Bob in his time, who would like to know him vicariously, to visit with this brave, committed and loving man, and learn more of what he was like as a husband, father, brother and friend, and of how completely unstereotypical he was.

The tone for this work was set long ago in the author's eulogy to his friend in a special RFK edition of *LOOK* magazine that he edited in June of 1968. It noted the Requiem Mass at Saint Patrick's Cathedral in New York City and the ride on the funeral train, an excruciating eight hours past endless clusters of mourning Americans, that brought him from New York to final rest on a hill overlooking Washington, D.C.:

At Arlington, we buried another Kennedy. Through the long funeral day, we felt more than grief. There was horror at the reality, and despair when we tried to tell our children that Americans are not a bloody people. We will never hear *The Battle Hymn of the Republic* without remembering. Nor will we forget the crowds on streets and station platforms, the majesty of the Mass, the widow's strength, the brotherhood of loss.

Of Robert Kennedy, we will recall a grin ten years too young, courage, earnestness and haste. He challenged Americans, frightened some and heartened millions. He had no halfhearted commitments, no idle interests, and no patience with those who did. Himself a man to whom almost everything seemed uphill, he identified with the downtrodden and the disadvantaged. He was a fighter, on myriad fronts, and yet he never attacked those weaker than he, only the powerful, the privileged. He moved in controversy, adored and despised, forever needing to be explained.

He was a magnificent man who always did his best.

A few days afterward, the author received a note from Ethel Kennedy that said in part:

Dear Warren,

I am grateful to you for so many kindnesses, but above all for your goodness of heart and understanding presence during these last difficult weeks.

It means so much to me to think of the many, many people who will read your warm words about Bobby and will know him as we did.

That is the purpose of the book: to tell the story of Robert Kennedy at Hickory Hill with the help of Ethel and others so that the people who read it "will know him as we did."

And know Ethel and their children as he did too.

When I Think of Bobby

Prologue

It is so quiet out there. Traffic hums and even roars at peak times along the Dolley Madison Boulevard, beyond the tree line at the rear of Hickory Hill. But the noise does not come through, oddly. The same at the front, where Chain Bridge Road sweeps past the low fence and its two unguarded, wide-open gates. It is so quiet. It does not seem possible that the big old, grayish-white house, atop a softly rolling hill that is more meadow than lawn, is fifteen minutes or less away from the heart of the District of Columbia. Or that it has seen so much triumph and tragedy, so much soaring hope and crushing pain.

Swinging the car into the driveway sets up a clatter. It is the cattle guard, a rough bridge made of four-inch, galvanized-iron pipes, that sounds like a freight train taking off every time it is rolled over. It is the most sophisticated warning that people in the house have that somebody has just entered the grounds. That, plus all the barking and yelping and howling the various dogs get into.

Up the short walk to the children-scarred steps at the front door, which is wide open behind a half-closed screen door as usual, I check for the sign on the lawn. It is still there: "Tres-passers Will Be Eaten."

The sign no longer carries any genuine threat. But there was a time when it had credibility. One of the children—proba-bly Bobby Jr., who early on was utterly certain he would grow up to be a zoologist or veterinarian, and acted accordingly—had put the warning there, half hoping it was true. Those were the days when Brumus ruled a booming menagerie of snakes, iguanas, a falcon, a coatimundi, horses, hamsters and, of course, dogs.

Brumus was a Newfoundland. But he was unlike any New-foundland anybody had ever seen or heard before. He was determinedly antisocial, with a single exception. Although he was prone to nip guests or one of the children, if they moved too quickly for his taste in touch football games, and even Ethel at times, he was unconditionally devoted to Robert Kennedy. He followed him around like a puppy. Bob often took him with him to work when he was Attorney General, to the horror of those at the office who were asked to walk him on their lunch hours. He certainly seemed capable of eating trespassers, or anybody else, especially on one of his frequent off days. Many were they who did not overly mourn Brumus's passing.

It is early autumn at Hickory Hill, and all the trees are responding on cue. The hickories, beeches, maples and oaks, which abound in this part of northern Virginia, are dropping their leaves with each rustling breeze. The weed trees, locusts and mimosas, hang on a little more stubbornly, as if acknowl-edging their underdog status and at the same time making a show of being a little tougher than the rest. This is the home, after all, of Bobby Kennedy, champion of the underdog, and his presence is still felt a generation after his death.

The twin oak just off the terrace at the back of the house towers majestically toward the clear sky. Suspended between its two trunks, where a treehouse used to be, is the Red Baron's World War I triplane. It is full-sized, but crude and swollen out of its true dimensions so that it is clearly a huge plaything. Set about twenty feet above the sloping lawn, it can be reached only by a wooden ladder that tilts precariously. The big toy is faded and tattered by years of weather and Kennedy rough-housing. Yet, as a splash of crimson marked ominously with a black Maltese cross, it is somehow menacing.

A steel cable runs from it to the ground about seventy yards away, where it anchors just to the side of the diving end of the swimming pool. A shuttle with handles hangs from the cable. A child, or a daring adult, could make that breakneck slide from tree to earth in considerably less than ten seconds—just as they do it at Fort Bragg, North Carolina, at the beginning of parachute training. Bob and the "big children" (that would be the four or five oldest of what would eventually be eleven Kennedy offspring) had brought the idea back from Fort Bragg after a visit. It was the headquarters of the U.S. Army's Special Forces, the celebrated Green Berets, who called themselves "Kennedy's Rifles" in honor of President Kennedy's revival of their unit in 1962 when he rejected U.S. Army objections ("one army, one uniform") and authorized them to wear their distinctive green beret.

Ethel Kennedy comes up the hill from the swimming pool, smiling and waving. She looks smaller these days, as she accepts her advancing years with increasing grace. Her body is still strong and vigorous, of course, what with all the tennis and ski-ing and sailing she still pursues. But she is beginning to spend more of her days out of the summer sun, for it has taken its toll in wrinkles around the eyes and mouth. The hair is silvery blond and youthful though, and Ethel maintains that little-girl look, as she probably always will. She is quieter too, and less hyperactive, and she does something she never used to do—she looks back in time a little and reminisces, even about Bobby, although she cannot seem to do that for very long. She does not appear to be racing so much now, reaching out fiercely for tomorrow, competitively, as if there was not enough future to go around and she wanted to make sure she got her share. She is looking about now, contemplating things, weighing and measuring. It suits her.

We talk about our children. With only two children, plus one granddaughter, I do not require much time to report on their activities. She is a grandmother several times over now, and we run the gamut: Kathleen's three, and Joe's twins, and Michael's little boy (another would soon be on the way). We talk of Courtney in New York, and of Kerry, Chris, Max and Douglas, and we touch obliquely on the drug problems of Bobby Jr. and David (Bobby's victory over drugs and the wrenching horror of David's death were, at that time, still to come). And, of course, we talked of Rory, the eleventh child, born six months after her father's assassination.

"Oh, kid, you won't believe it!" Ethel says. "She went and had ten teeth extracted all at once—ten!"

And where was she? Upstairs, lying down?

"No, no! She's out at the airport with the others, picking up some friends," Ethel says. "I guess she's like Bobby. Low threshold of pain—or is it high threshold? High, I guess. Anyway, she can take a lot of pain, like Bobby. Not like me. I'd be yelling and screaming and running around. . . ."

I laugh, and I look at her closely, to see if she is teasing. But the expression on her face is of pure innocence. She really means that she could not stand much pain. And this from a woman who had borne eleven children—several by Caesarian section—and who had suffered with ennobling dignity through the deaths of her parents and brother in air crashes, and the assassinations of her husband's brother and of her husband himself, almost before her very eyes, and more. The Robert Burns poem, about seeing ourselves as others see us, flashes into my head. And I chuckle at the idea that a toothache—or even ten toothaches at once—could cause Ethel Kennedy to go "yelling and screaming and running around."

As it had many times before, it came home to me how much it had meant to Bob to have Ethel backing him up, and the children, and the solid security of Hickory Hill, well away from the arenas of downtown Washington, a five-and-a-half-acre oasis of nothing more complicated than whooping cough and measles and a broken limb, perhaps, or who was going to be on whose side in the touch football game. Bob had sought to tell me several times how he felt about this, but he was a shy and private man. His explanations at such times almost always came out halting and elliptical, and I remember especially one explanation, which, at the end, he summarized simply:

"Anyway, most people with our resources would hire a lot of people to take care of the children while they went off and did something else. We do it the other way around. We hire people to do that something else, and that frees us up for the time that we can spend with the children."

Often since then, I have thought about how much sense that made, and of how few parents nowadays follow anything like it. And I have wondered too, whether Bob might have figured the odds were so great against his living a normal three score and ten years that he had better hurry to store up memories of who and what he was in the minds and hearts of his children, to guide them after he was gone. He would have snorted at such an idea as too fuzzy-headed and romantic, but I am certain it would nevertheless have occurred to him. He often hid his profundities, and he particularly labored against any perceptions of himself as some kind of self-effacing hero. On the business of his being the "family S.O.B.," a kind of official naysayer and doer of the grubby chores, especially of being a lightning rod to draw off criticisms of his brother in the White House, he would grin and deny it, feebly. He accepted the role without complaint, but he never enjoyed it, and, once, as we sat side by side in a campaign airplane, he said to me:

"Any president bears so much responsibility that, when something goes wrong, somebody should move forward and take the blame or accept the heat if something unpopular must be done. People want the president kept as a higher authority to appeal to, and, if someone else attracts the anger and draws the fire, that's all to the good."

Ethel and I continue talking as we walk around the outside of her great old clapboard house. We pass the sweeping lawn, where the touch football games used to be held, and I think of all the games there, sometimes among world-class, professional athletes, sometimes among little children and their mothers, and sometimes both. A game was a game, and, almost always, Bobby Kennedy was in it, regardless of its quality, and trying to run it. I recall that Ethel once told me Bob usually went out and tossed the ball around with whoever was available, children or guests or whatever, from 7 to 7:30 in the morning, before going off to work.

On the lawn now, some younger Kennedys are chasing around after each other, giggling and falling down in a heap. I point and say, "That's where Brumus bit me."

Ethel protests, "Oh, he didn't!"

"Twice," I say.

We laugh, because we both know it is God's own truth.

Not to be outdone, and because a Kennedy always tries to get in the last word, she adds:

"You probably deserved it."

1

Hickory Hill

It was early 1957 and young Robert Kennedy was riding high. Politically, he had tasted both victory and defeat. He had helped his brother John get elected to the U.S. House of Representatives and then to the U.S. Senate. But they had also lost a bid to get John Kennedy on the 1956 Democratic ticket as Adlai E. Stevenson's vice presidential running mate. As a budding public figure himself, Bob had escaped from an uncomfortable stint with Senator Joseph R. McCarthy's Communist hunters and had come into his own as the tough-questioning general counsel for the Senate Permanent Subcommittee on Investigations, applauded for exposing the labor racketeering of Dave Beck, James Hoffa and others.

The forces of monumental social change were stirring in the United States at that time, some quietly and some with explosive passion. Jack Kerouac published On the Road, *the book that defined the beatnik movement and became its bible. Congress passed the first civil rights legislation since Reconstruction, a voting rights law, and, down in Arkansas, Little Rock's previously all-white Central High School erupted in violence when nine black students sought to enter under a court order. President Eisenhower sent federal troops to enforce the order. The battle for civil rights in the South had begun.*

*   *   *

The car rattled across the loose pipes of the cattle-guard bridge and the children started cheering at the same time. They yelled as loud as they could and until they ran out of breath, and then they took another breath and yelled some more. It was Klaxon-horn cheering, all voices merging into one continuous blast. At first, Bob and Ethel, leading the way in a separate automobile, grinned and looked at each other. But, in a moment, they couldn't stand it anymore and they were cheering too.

They had hoped for it and talked about it and planned for it and here it was at last. They were through with bouncing from one rented house to another, a half dozen and more since they had taken up residence in Washington. Hickory Hill was now their base of operations, their headquarters, their safe haven, their own center of the universe. They had a home at last.

"Welcome to Hickory Hill!" Bob said quietly, almost to himself, and he stopped his car at the top of the rainbow arc of a driveway, where the brick walkway leads to the front door. The door was wide open, as it was to be most of the time thereafter.

There was more yelling, and shouts of "Let's get out!" and the like coming from the car behind him bearing the children and their nursemaid, Ena Bernard, who had brought them by train from Hyannis Port in Massachusetts. Bob and Ethel had flown up from Palm Beach, Florida, and met them at Washington's Union Depot.

Kathleen, perhaps asserting a right as firstborn or more likely because she was the biggest and most excited, was the first to burst from the car. Joe, who was four, and Bobby, who was three, tumbled out too and ran after her. So did David, barely toddling at two, but Mary Courtney, still a babe in arms, stayed behind with her parents. Kathleen led the others in running around and around on the grass. There was far more lawn at Hickory Hill than in the combined total at all the other houses they had lived in, rented for a year or so in Washington's Georgetown neighborhood when they returned from summers on Cape Cod.

Three dogs chased after them, barking and jumping, celebrating their reunion with the children. They had been brought on ahead from the Kennedy compound at Hyannis Port, and—a very pleasant surprise—so had some horses. Kathleen, the family's prime lover of horses, was ecstatic. Hickory Hill meant room enough for horses and, at the first chance, she made a beeline for the stable at the back of the house as fast as her six-year-old legs could carry her.

Thus did the Robert F. Kennedys, then numbering seven, arrive at Hickory Hill on January 13, 1957. It was Bob's idea, more or less, to settle his growing family into something like Hickory Hill. He had strong patriarchal support, father Joseph Patrick Kennedy virtually insisting that son John sell the estate he had just bought in McLean, Virginia, to son Robert.

"You look like the one who's going to have all the kids," he told Bob. "You may as well get a big place now and develop it into something that suits you and your needs."

Bob Kennedy was just then embarking on a long stretch of work as chief counsel of the Senate Select Committee on Improper Activities in the Labor or Management Field, informally called the Senate Rackets Committee. It was headed by Democratic Senator John L. McClellan of Arkansas, and Bob's brother John, as a Democratic Senator from Massachusetts, was a member. Bob knew, from having participated in other Senate investigations, what to expect.

"I'm going to be gone a lot," he told Ethel. "I'm going to be going to work before the children are up, and I'll be coming home after they're asleep. I'll be traveling a lot. But, whenever I can, I'll take some time off to be with you and the children. That will be our time. And we won't let any office work or anything else get in the way, if we can help it."

As it turned out, Bob's public responsibilities did indeed intrude on life at Hickory Hill often. In the beginning, he and Ethel worked determinedly at carving out private "quality" time for themselves and the children. But it was not easy. The public time and the private time began to overlap, more and more as Bob's activities and responsibilities grew.

Sometimes, invasions from the outside world were frightening, as when rough-voiced callers telephoned threats against the children, or when burly men in tight dark suits drove slowly past Hickory Hill in big black automobiles. Yet Ethel managed to create an atmosphere of vitality and security as her growing family settled into its splendid new home. Jacqueline Kennedy had recently decorated the old place, but Ethel pitched into doing it all over, in her favorite pinks and greens and yellows, and trying, with occasional success, to make it more livable for all and at least somewhat child-proof and pet-proof.

Kennedy children and their pets, including the ubiquitous Brumus, wandered around and through the house, and even made excursions to Bob's office in downtown Washington.

Or Bob brought his office home with him, books and papers stacked around in various rooms, with associates working at them while Kennedy children played all around, squabbling or laughing about something, but always making a good deal of noise, and always to a chorus of dogs barking a harsh obbligato without letup.

Bobby and Ethel came to Hickory Hill from opposite directions. For her, it was simply the chance to recreate the kind of Rock of Gibraltar home she had grown up in, loving, comfortable, solid, safe, and secure. For him, it was the end of what he would sometimes call, when in a dark mood, an awful lot of wandering around. Born in Massachusetts, he was moved to New York when barely a year old, and then to London, where his father was the American ambassador, then back again to Massachusetts. There were splendid homes for him and his family at every stop, of course, but none providing him with the sense of solid roots that would solace an innately shy and lonely little boy.

Bob's brother John had bought the big, handsome old house and its sprawling grounds in early 1954, a few months after John's marriage in September of 1953 to the elegant Jacqueline Bouvier. A century and a half old, the house had high ceilings and crystal chandeliers and a respectable history: it had been General George Brinton McClellan's Civil War headquarters, and a recent owner had been Supreme Court Justice Robert H. Jackson.

Bob admired Jackson but had a low opinion of McClellan. True to character, he shared President Lincoln's exasperation with the hesitant "Little Mac," unsurpassed at raising and training troops but loath to commit them to battle. "McClellan didn't press," Bob said with a grimace, his trademark in discussing anything he found distasteful.

Jackie had spent a good deal of time and attention on preparing a place at Hickory Hill for her firstborn. A carefully designed and superbly furnished nursery was the result. But the baby was born dead in Newport. At the time, Jack was in Europe, resting after his unsuccessful run at the 1956 Democratic convention against Senator Estes Kefauver of Tennessee for the vice presidential slot on Presidential nominee Adlai Stevenson's ticket. It took several days for word to reach him. In the meantime, Bob went to the hospital immediately. He was the first person Jackie saw at her bedside when she regained consciousness. And it was he, she later learned, who made the arrangements for burying the baby, a girl.

Only a few days later, on September 9, 1956, Ethel gave birth to her fifth child, a girl, christened Mary Courtney. And it was unmistakably clear that the little house they were then renting in Washington's Georgetown neighborhood was not going to do any longer. Jackie's pain at the contemplation of Hickory Hill and its lovingly created nursery would not do either.

In early 1957, Bob paid his brother $125,000 for Hickory Hill, exactly what Jack had bought it for. Ethel consulted professional decorators as well as close friends whose taste she trusted. Sarah Davis, Anita Fay, Susie Markham and a few others kicked in with ideas for Ethel and Hickory Hill.

For Bob, there was not much time then for Hickory Hill,

other than to talk over with Ethel each step of the transformation that would make the place their home. He had brought his political education up to date by traveling around with the Stevenson campaign, making extensive and detailed notes that told how to run a presidential campaign and how not to. And, as 1957 got under way, he was putting together a staff of scores of investigators, with stars such as Pierre Salinger and Carmine Bellino and Walter Sheridan, for an assault on labor racketeering that would keep him away from home for longer hours than ever, make him a national celebrity in his own right, and even bring threats of an acid attack on his children's eyes. Bob refused to discuss such things with the press, his staff, and even his family. And he refused to take much more than minimal precautions.

Like an occupying army, the seven Kennedys moved in, and the legend began. At the rate they were producing babies, Bob and Ethel agreed, only half-jokingly, that Hickory Hill's fourteen rooms might soon be overcrowded too.

They certainly expected more children. Noting his own parents had nine children, Bob joked, "Four to go for a tie, five to win." But he actually was more resigned than competitive. He and Ethel agreed, "We'll take whatever God sends."

That, in fact, was a magical phrase, the code by which Bob and Ethel let the children know an addition was on the way. It was a simple trick. At the dinner table, after saying grace, Bob or Ethel called down blessings on all present—"God bless Mommy and Daddy and Kathleen and Joseph and Bobby and David and Courtney"—and then tacked on, "and whatever God sends." That never failed to create an explosion of squeals and yells.

"Oh, when?"

"A new sister!"

"No, a brother!"

There was nothing else for Bob and Ethel to do amid the commotion of crowding around Ethel and everybody talking at once, but to sit there and beam. They knew what would happen, and it did. It was another precious moment, another family snapshot, for the memory book.

For the children, it took no time at all to turn what had been "Uncle Jack's place" into their own. All that space and all that grass and all those trees. It was a far cry from the cramped quarters in Georgetown. And, with Ethel tolerating their antics and Bob slyly cheering them on, they made the most of it.

For Kathleen from the age of six on, the best times were with the horses, especially when Bob rode along with her. He really had no particular liking for horses and, in fact, started out a little skittish of them. But, urged on by Kathleen, he learned to ride and, after that, he rode with the same daredevil abandon he brought to football, rafting, and any other sport he attempted, eventually including mountain climbing.

Collecting blue ribbons in horse shows would come later, but nothing else ever approached the thrill of riding pell-mell alongside her father down the highway near Hickory Hill. There was little traffic where they rode, along the wooded outskirts of the Central Intelligence Agency headquarters, and, usually at a challenge from Bob, they would race. They would gallop as fast as their mounts could go, sometimes almost out of control, laughing riotously all the way.

"You were terrible," Bob, typically, once needled her at the barn. "You were out of control."

"I was out of control?" She was genuinely piqued. "You were out of control, Dad! You panicked!"

It was the worst insult to accuse a Kennedy of panic. They argued like that and, as usual, that led to pushing and shoving and, finally, a "tickle-tumble," as they called it, one small child and one overgrown one rolling around in the grass and exchanging terrible threats and mock punches. Any other Kennedys who were around were welcome to join in. They usually did, to make it a regular Donnybrook that left everybody all laughed out and tearfully exhausted.

Sometimes, Bob would do a curious thing with the boys, although never with the girls. In the midst of a tickle-tumble or other roughhousing, he would slap them in the face, rather smartly. If the little boy cried, Bob would hug him and coo to him, but not in a coddling way. He would say softly, "Hush now, a Kennedy never cries." And the game would go on.

Once, a guest, watching such a scene, suggested to Bob that perhaps he was too rough on so small a child. He replied, again in his soft way:

"No, they have to get used to getting hit. It's going to happen out there in the world. They have to learn to take it and go on, to get used to getting hit so it's no surprise, no shock they can't sustain."

2

Bob

While Robert Kennedy was getting his life together, America was regrouping too, turning back to its domestic agenda after leading the Allies to victory in World War II. But the Soviet Union stayed on a war footing and the Cold War replaced the shooting war. It was the time of the Marshall Plan of economic aid to rebuild all of Europe, and of the Truman Doctrine to contain communism in Greece and Turkey. President Truman won his first struggle against Joseph Stalin with an airlift that broke the Berlin Blockade. He followed with the North Atlantic Treaty Organization to shield Europe against the continuing Soviet threat. The United Nations, formed to foster international amity, as one of its first acts fought a war, under U.S. leadership, to repel Communist incursion into South Korea.

At home, President Truman wrestled with demobilization, housing, road building, McCarthyism, restive labor unions largely restrained by the war, and other swords-into-plowshares challenges. His speech to the Japanese Peace Treaty Conference in San Francisco inaugurated transcontinental television. The first hydrogen bomb was exploded. USS Nautilus, the first atomic submarine, took to the ways. Jackie Robinson joined the Brooklyn Dodgers as the first black player in major league base-ball. J. D. Salinger's Catcher in the Rye *was published, and so was* The Kinsey Report on Sexuality in the Human Male.

President Eisenhower, Truman's successor, gave aid but no troops to the French fight against Indochina insurgents, genesis of the Vietnam War that was to plague three presidents after him. The Supreme Court declared public school segregation unconstitutional and ordered integration "with all deliberate speed." In Montgomery, Alabama, Rosa Parks refused to move to the back of the bus. The stage was set for the bloody civil rights clashes of the 1960s.

Bob Kennedy caught the red-eye flight back from his secret mission to Seattle. He was accustomed to sleeping on long airplane rides, but this time he was restless and wakeful, the excitement of his clandestine undertaking still with him. There was no chance of sleep while the details raced through his mind. He had just completed another trip to the West Coast (registering at a hotel as "Mr. Rogers," a puckish borrowing, he confessed, from children's television) as chief counsel for the Senate Select Committee on Improper Activities in the Labor or Management Field, headed by Democratic Senator John L. McClellan of Arkansas. He was excited because his long, mostly undercover investigation of the powerful Teamsters Union and its international president, Dave Beck, seemed at last to be bearing fruit.

Now, on his way back to his family, he faced a serious problem, as critical to him on the home front as bringing Dave Beck to justice. It was Christmastime and the end of yet another trip, a double reason for presents for the children, and he had none.

Worse, he well knew how serious Ethel was about Christmas. It was her favorite holiday, and she had moved their entire brood from Hickory Hill to Hyannis Port in Massachusetts to celebrate it at the Kennedy compound there.

Arriving at the Boston airport, he went immediately to the newsstand gift shop. He gathered an armload of trinkets, but he was far from satisfied. And then he saw it, the perfect gift, just outrageous enough to score big with everybody and win some forgiveness for his frequent and untimely absences on business.

"I'm sorry," the clerk said. "It's not for sale. It's part of the display for our line of Christmas cards."

"But Christmas is just about over," Bob protested. "You have no more use for it after today."

And so he bought it and, lugging it over to the telephones on the wall, he called Ethel and asked her to send a car for him at the airport.

"Why don't you just get a cab?" Ethel asked.

"I have my reasons," Bob said. "Please send a car, and no questions asked. And, look, I know it's cold, but make sure you send the convertible."

Mystified but dutiful, Ethel complied. And that is why she and the children, tingling with cold and anticipation, fell to howling when Bob drove up hugging a bigger-than-life Santa Claus—not a cardboard cutout, but a three-dimensional, stuffed Santa standing six feet tall in his red-and-white velveteen suit and black leatherette belt and boots. When you plugged him in, he waved hello and his head waggled.

The big Santa was the hit of that Christmas, of course. All the other presents that Ethel had carefully gathered over several weeks of shopping had to take second place to the minor miracle Bob had produced on the spur of the moment.

When Bob and Ethel and the children returned to Hickory Hill, the Santa moved with them. It wound up in the basement playroom, where it hung around for years, hugged and rough-housed, growing more faded and more tattered, until it simply disappeared. One day it was there and the next it was gone. Whatever happened to it remains a mystery.

Bob loved stunts like that. They appealed to the Peter Pan in him that refused to grow up. They allied him with the people he understood best and trusted the most, children. And they gave him respite from the crushing tasks he set for himself in the world outside Hickory Hill—jailing the Dave Becks and Jimmy

Hoffas, enforcing civil rights for the victims of bigotry, running campaigns for the world's greatest political offices (and doubling as the no-sayer and official S.O.B.), and all the rest.

On the day in January 1961 that he was sworn in as Attorney General, Bob was an exuberant Pied Piper leading Ethel and their children, then totaling seven, to the White House for the ceremony. Everybody was dressed to the nines, Bob and Ethel in brand-new finery, the girls in fluffy, frilly dresses and the boys, as Nanny Ena Bernard remembers proudly, "all of them in gray, pretty and neat—they always dressed up nicer than their cousins."

As soon as the swearing-in was over and the last photograph taken, Bob led the six oldest children on a tour of the White House for a firsthand lesson in history. Kerry, a little over one, stayed with Ethel and the other adults.

Kathleen, the oldest at almost ten, and Courtney wanted to see "the room with all the First Ladies' pictures in it." Joe, Bobby, David and little Michael, not quite three, went along so they could stay close to their father.

Leading the way downstairs, Bob eschewed the steps, sat on the banister rail and slid the whole way down. There was a burst of yelling and, with Kathleen in the lead and Michael right behind her, follow the leader—all the Kennedys slid down the banister rail. Ena shrieked.

In those staid precincts, the marbled and paneled walls echoed with the raucous shouts and laughter of Bob Kennedy and his children. It was perhaps the noisiest the place had been since Franklin D. Roosevelt's grandchildren played hide-and-seek there.

"Oh, Mr. Kennedy!" Ena cried. "Sliding down the banister at the White House! Imagine it! I can't believe it! Mr. Kennedy, you'll never grow up!"

He grinned even more broadly. And she knew she had spoken the truth. Part of him would always remain a boy. As she said later:

"When it came to playing with his children, he never did grow up."

Of a sudden, somebody said, "Somebody's coming!"

All fell silent. The children lined up, shoulder to shoulder, pressed against the wall, listening wide-eyed to the echoing footfalls draw closer. Bob too.

Around the corner came a man in a dark suit. His face lit up as soon as he saw that lineup, no longer pushing and yelling but silent, subdued, correct, angelic.

"Oh my, what beautiful children!" he smiled, patting a head or two before moving on. "So neat! And so nice! What nice children!"

Bob rolled his eyes. A moment earlier, he had had a pack of wild ruffians in tow. Suddenly, they were nice, beautiful children.

"Who was that man?" somebody asked.

"Hubert Humphrey," Bob said.

Indeed it was, the same Hubert Humphrey whose 1960 presidential ambitions had collapsed in West Virginia's primary a few months earlier, crushed by the "Kennedy juggernaut" that Bob directed at him. But then the sunny Humphrey could never hold a grudge. He found much of the world nice, perhaps because, in truth, there was no fairer description of the man himself.

Few in public life regarded Bob Kennedy as nice by the time he got to Hickory Hill. He long since had given up any burning concern for approbation outside of his family and his conscience. He saw himself as a born underdog, despairing of ever matching the dash and daring of older brothers Joe and John. His solution was to aim high and try harder. As David Hackett, a friend since adolescence, saw it:

"He was neither a natural athlete nor a natural student nor a natural success with girls and had no natural gift for popularity. Nothing came easily for him. What he had was a set of handicaps and a fantastic determination to overcome them. The handicaps made him redouble his effort."

He knew the odds against him, for example, when he went out for football at Harvard. At 5 foot 9 and 155 pounds, he made very little impression on Dick Harlow, Harvard's head football coach. He reported as an end when Harvard was enjoying the biggest bumper crop of outstanding ends in its athletic program's history.

Kenneth O'Donnell, whose father was football coach at Holy Cross and whose older brother was captain of the 1946 Harvard team and who would be captain himself the following year, recalled the situation years later:

"The GI Bill after World War II allowed even the poorest of boys to seek an education in our best universities. Harvard was overflowing with the finest collection of athletes to be found anywhere. The Harvard squad was inundated with transfers from all over—most of the boys had played one or two years at Notre Dame, Wisconsin and so forth. Because of Bobby's size, the coaches consigned him to sixth or seventh squad. In college football, that's the end. The varsity coaches never see you again."

But they saw Bob Kennedy. He made it a rule to show up on the practice field an hour early and stay an hour late. In scrimmages, O'Donnell recalled, "He'd come in like a wild Indian . . . If you were blocking Bobby, you'd knock him down and he'd get up and you'd knock him down again, and he would be up and going after the play. He never let up."

Soon, Bob was promoted to the varsity and the wisecracks about lack of size and speed dried up. He was invited into the Varsity Club, and he adopted the routine of the campus jock, loving every minute.

"I didn't go to class very much," he confessed later, and his grades showed it. He was on probation for mediocre marks until the spring of 1947.

He was elected to the Spee Club, like his brothers Joseph and John, but he avoided it angrily after another Irish Catholic was blackballed. He also got into a row at the Catholic St.

Benedict Center, opposing Father Leonard Feeney's tirades there that contended that only Catholics could enter Heaven and that Harvard was a "pest-hole" of Jews and atheists. Bob's fight with Father Feeney upset his mother, although she could draw comfort later when Boston's Cardinal Cushing suspended the priest in 1949 and the Vatican excommunicated him in 1953.

In 1947, Bob's senior year, he was an established varsity member. Harlow told another player, Nicholas Rodis: "Bobby is the toughest boy pound for pound that I have coached since Bobby Green." Green had been captain of one of Harlow's greatest prewar football teams and also an outstanding boxer.

Rodis knew what O'Donnell and their teammates and coaches knew, that Bob was never going to be fast enough to be exceptional on offense. But, in those days of playing both offense and defense, his "wild Indian" charges on defense more than made up for his deficiencies at catching passes.

Yet, he did manage a touchdown, on a pass from O'Donnell, in Harvard's opening-day rout of Western Maryland, 47 to 0. But the glory for both of them was short-lived. At practice the following week, O'Donnell and Kennedy were scrimmaging side by side, and they were doing so poorly that Coach Harlow came over to give them special attention.

"We were missing block after block," O'Donnell recalled. "The coach was raging at me, and I was raging at Bobby. After about half an hour, Bob collapsed on the field. He had been playing with a broken leg all that time, which was so indicative of the determination and desire that was to motivate his whole life. That ended his football career, although he did play in the Yale game to earn his letter."

It was Coach Harlow who decided Bob should have his letter, the first in the family since Bob's father won his crimson "H" in baseball. Bob sat on the bench, disconsolately watching the Yale-Harvard game, in which one had to play to earn a letter. His leg was not totally healed and he had little hope of playing. Just before the last play of the game, Harlow shouted, "Kennedy!"

Thunderstruck, Bobby hobbled in.

When the whistle blew and the hitting stopped, there he was, in the midst of the melee, involved in the tackle despite everything. He had done it after all.

Teammate Samuel Adams was not surprised. He had gone to Milton Academy in Massachusetts and, together with David Hackett, was best friends with Bob. Hackett chose to pass up Harvard for McGill University in Canada, but Adams stayed with Bob through Harvard. Hackett was by far the most gifted athlete, superb in several sports. After serving as an Army paratrooper in World War II and then starring in football and hockey in Canada, he rejoined Bob in Washington.

Both Adams and Hackett remember how strange Bob seemed when they first met him at Milton. They, like the majority of the boys at that tradition-bound prep school, were White Anglo-Saxon Protestant to the eyebrows. Bobby had attended mostly Catholic parochial schools up to that time, a total of six in ten years. His first boarding school was St. Paul's in Concord, New Hampshire. But his mother found its Episcopalianism daunting ("The Protestant Bible was read at different times . . . [and] it was for this reason that I withdrew Bobby."). She enrolled him in Portsmouth Priory near Newport, Rhode Island, where the Benedictines who ran it provided prayers twice daily, Mass three times a week and High Mass on Sundays. After three years, he transferred to Milton.

"Now he was in a new environment," Adams recalled. "A handful of Catholics, two or three Jews, and the rest Protestants, predominantly of Anglo-Saxon background, made up the student body of 'non-sectarian' Milton Academy."

Hackett remembered down to the last button how different Bob Kennedy looked that first day they met:

"His clothes were all wrong, I thought. There was nothing really wrong with them. It's just that they were not like our clothes. They were different. He was different. He talked differently, and he held himself differently, and you knew right away that there was something here we ought to be looking into."

Sam Adams was taken aback by the intensity of Bobby's approach to football. He went at it so seriously, Sam recalled, that it seemed to be a life-or-death struggle for him on every play, in practice as much as on game day.

"My first insight into Bobby's character" was the way Adams described what he saw when they both worked out in the second-string backfield at Milton in late 1942.

"Bobby ran every practice play and tackled and blocked dummies as if he were in a hard-fought game," Sam said. "To another sixteen-year-old kid, this gung-ho attitude seemed a little weird. But, gradually, I became aware of another characteristic of Bobby's which I admired most—his ability to ridicule himself and his efforts and still go all out. Unfortunately, for Bobby's popularity at Milton Academy, his self-deprecating humor was mostly confined to his close friends, of whom he had two, as I recall, Dave Hackett and myself."

Bob was no more popular at Harvard than at Milton, and for the same reasons. To begin with, he picked his friends, not the other way around. Also, he never had difficulty settling his priorities. At Milton, he had two friends, Sam and Dave, and at Harvard he had the football team. One was an extension of the other, and both were all he needed to meet the standards of toughness—physical, mental and moral—that he had set for himself. These were higher even than those he felt his father had set for him, and that was important to him, like showing up an hour early for practice and staying an hour later.

Both at Milton and at Harvard, those whom Bob had not sought out and anointed as friends found him rude, standoffish, contentious and dull. Small wonder that, for those to whom he showed only this side, whatever time it took to escape his company was too long.

He did not like cruel or dirty jokes, for instance, and he refused to respond when one was told in his presence. He caused many a budding comedian to feel foolish by refusing to acknowledge snide innuendos about sex or race, not even with a good-natured grunt or groan, as some others did when smut or ethnic slurs made them uncomfortable.

Part of the price that Sam and Dave had to pay for their friendship with Bob, aside from defending him against constant criticism from their other friends, was going to church. The Catholic church nearest to Milton was at least a mile and a half away. Like so many Protestant New Englanders, Sam and Dave had a deep suspicion of Catholics and what Sam called their "religion of chants, incense, beads and medals."

The two boys, sometimes together with Bob and sometimes one on one, had plenty of chances to seal their friendship with him on the long walks to and from church. He rarely missed a Sunday or holy day of obligation, and they came to understand the nature of his faith.

"On these walks, we talked about all those things boys talk about," Sam recalled, "but I also came to realize that the incense, beads and medals which I saw as things of superstition were only symbols. His absolute faith in God also gave him faith in himself and appeared to make him oblivious of his lack of popularity among many of his classmates. What was so remarkable to me was that, despite the treatment that he was sometimes accorded, he cared about Milton. He talked, even then, about the importance of making a contribution."

Bob's contribution to Harvard football cost him dearly, academically. The Harvard and Yale law schools told him his grades were below their standards. He considered, and even applied for, admission to Harvard Business School, and he joked with his sister Patricia about looking into Georgetown University Dental School. The University of Virginia, after telling him his undergraduate record made it "unlikely" he would be accepted there without a high score on the Law Scholastic Aptitude Test, finally agreed to let him in.

First, there was a grand tour of Europe and the Middle East, a graduation present from his father, who wondered to friends if Bob would be able to overcome the "handicap" of having to follow the brilliance of big brothers Joe and John. Joseph P. Kennedy, through his European connections, opened doors for his third son, but there was a kicker. He had him accredited to the *Boston Post*. Thus, Bob was no idle tourist but a journalist faced with the discipline of recording what he saw, organizing his facts and articulating them in readable form.

Bob did, in fact, file stories from England, France, Germany, Egypt, Israel and elsewhere, improving his knowledge and powers of observation. After Copenhagen, his education had nowhere to go but up. He met his sisters there, and they dragged him off to museums to see Danish art. "I never even knew there was any," he wrote his mother.

As it seemed always to be with the Kennedys, tragedy intruded on the joy of the trip. While Bob was in Italy, his sister Kathleen Hartington died in an airplane crash. Alastair Forbes called her "the best and the brightest-eyed of all Kennedys." Down with jaundice in Italy, Bob missed the funeral but visited her grave later at Chatsworth, England. He also went to the grave of her husband, Lord Hartington, near the farmhouse in Belgium where he fell leading an infantry patrol in 1944, soon after Bob's brother Joe died on a bombing mission. It was a grim time for young Bob and his family, with Joe, Kick and Billy gone, Jack hospitalized off and on for injuries suffered when a Japanese destroyer sank his PT-109 patrol boat, and sister Rosemary, her mental impairment hopelessly severe, finally placed in a facility in Wisconsin overseen by nuns.

Bobby checked into Charlottesville with some trepidation. He approached the study of law determinedly, listening intently and studying hard. One accomplishment was a paper on the reserve powers of the U.S. Constitution under the Ninth and Tenth amendments. Another was an essay attacking President Franklin D. Roosevelt's concessions to Soviet dictator Joseph Stalin at Yalta. But, he truly shined in his final year, as president of the Student Legal Forum, which he revitalized.

Bob brought his father to the campus as a Forum speaker and his brother John, the new U.S. Senator from Mas-

sachusetts, plus an array, one after the other, of his father's cele-
brated friends. They included Thurman Arnold, Senator Joseph
R. McCarthy of Wisconsin, Supreme Court Justice William O.
Douglas, columnist Arthur Krock of the *New York Times* and
James M. Landis, who had served with Bobby's father on the
Securities and Exchange Commission in the 1930s.

It took some doing, but he prevailed in having the United
Nations' Ralph Bunche as a speaker on Bunche's no-segrega-
tion terms. He convinced the law school's sympathetic dean,
Colgate Darden, that Dr. Bunche's lecture was an educational
event and thus, by new federal law, had to be racially inte-
grated. It was a moving event for Bunche, in those early days,
to talk to an audience in Virginia that was one-third black and
sitting wherever it chose.

Bob did well at law, despite his early misgivings, especially
in constitutional and labor law. He was graduated fifty-sixth in
a class of 125 in June of 1951, the first of the children of
Joseph and Rose Kennedy to have a profession.

In the meantime, Bob had rediscovered Ethel. By the end
of 1948, he was courting her with the intensity he had once
lavished on football. He would visit Manhattanville College in
New York City on weekends, and they would drive downtown
for a movie or a Broadway play and perhaps dancing at El
Morocco or the Stork Club. Or they would spend the weekend
with her family in Greenwich. Occasionally, she would visit him
in Charlottesville.

They seemed deeply in love, both of them. And Jean the
matchmaker and everybody else concerned started figuring out
possible wedding dates. Rose Kennedy expressed misgivings
about her son's marrying while still in law school, although she
was delighted with his choice of Ethel.

But then, disaster struck. Ethel confided to Jean that she
had been having second thoughts about marriage, to Bobby or
to anybody else, and even about the whole concept of secular
life.

"I wonder," she told Bobby's sister, "if God really means for me to dedicate my life to Him. Sometimes, I feel a very strong impulse and a longing to take the veil and serve God completely in that way."

Bob was flabbergasted. Walking the beach at Hyannis Port on Cape Cod in Massachusetts, he confessed to Jean that he was completely stymied. He was sure he could compete against any other suitors Ethel might attract, but this was different.

"How can I fight God?" he asked, with aching seriousness.

3

Ethel

Joseph P. Kennedy designated his oldest son, Joseph Jr., as his proxy to fulfill his dream of a political career culminating in the White House. When Joe died a hero in World War II, the mantle fell to the next oldest, John, and he began by running for the U.S. House of Representatives from Massachusetts in 1946. Bob Kennedy, out of the Navy and enrolled at Harvard, reported for duty in the family enterprise. Dismissed at first as too callow and inarticulate, he hung around until he became an asset, as his brother, having won election, grudgingly conceded. It was America's first full postwar year, the year the Philippines was given its independence. For Ethel Kennedy, though, it was a year of decision, indecision, decision, indecision . . .

On the one hand, Ethel Skakel wanted to get married, and to Robert Francis Kennedy. On the other, she didn't want to get married to Robert Kennedy or anybody else. She really felt she should become a nun. It was a terrible dilemma, and it was driving her to distraction.

There was another thing. Ethel had a bit of a guilty conscience about maneuvering Bobby into proposing marriage. After all, she had gone after him like a general drawing up detailed war plans and then deploying forces skillfully to carry out that strategy. She had stolen Bob from her older sister Patricia.

Actually, Pat hardly noticed. And Bobby was barely aware of what was going on, not unusual for a young man of twenty making his first serious sortie into the dating arena. Pat hardly noticed because she was quite indifferent toward the serious young fellow. She found him annoyingly shy and more than a little dull. If Ethel had been less devious in her campaign and come right out and explained the way things were to Pat, she undoubtedly would have had her sister's enthusiastic help.

But Ethel had set her cap for Bobby, from the moment she first saw him. Her seventeen-year-old heart leaped at the look and sound of him. Even his shyness and lack of dash, exactly what deterred Pat, drew her to him. And, from the beginning, she had Bob's sister Jean, her close friend and roommate at Manhattanville College of the Sacred Heart, then in upper Manhattan, urging her on like a cheerleader.

Jean was quiet and withdrawn too, like Bob. She often confessed she would like to be more outgoing and even a touch flamboyant, like Ethel. She delighted in the antics of the supercharged Ethel, and she admired and liked her very much. She was sure, knowing Bob as well as she did, that he would like Ethel too, and vice versa. And so she talked up what a wonderful pair they would make, lobbying them both, Ethel when she was at school and Bobby when she was at home. Quiet and withdrawn, yes, but Jean was not above playing puppeteer with two of the people she most loved in the world.

It was 1945, and World War II had just ended. Ethel had come bounding out of Greenwich Academy in Greenwich, Connecticut, determined to study harder and make better grades at Manhattanville. But she also cherished her sense of independence, and she vowed not to lose that. She kept both promises to herself. She did well at Manhattanville, especially in

English and dramatics, and won attention too, as an athlete.

The Manhattanville yearbook pictured her: "An excited hoarse voice, a shriek, a peal of screaming laughter, the flash of shirttails, a tousled brown head—Ethel! Her face at one moment a picture of utter guilelessness and at the next alive with mischief."

The nuns remember her also as "mischievous," and as one who earned her share of demerits. Once, the demerit book itself disappeared. And it was no secret who had shoved it down the incinerator chute. With this record of demerits missing, Ethel and all the other girls listed in the book were freed for the weekend and their weekend dates.

Still, the faith that was to sustain her through life's later tests already was there. The nuns saw immediately that, along with the restless rebellion that led to girlish pranks, Ethel had a genuine piety that expressed itself in faithful attendance at daily Mass and Holy Communion. The watchful sisters of the Sacred Heart smiled at this omen of the good woman she would become.

"Noisy and a handful," said one nun who had taught her. "But a good girl, a real good girl."

Jean the matchmaker picked the ski slopes of Mont Tremblant in Canada as the place and the Christmas holidays of 1945 as the time to introduce her brother and her roommate. Ethel told Jean it was love at first sight for her. She wondered that she had managed a breezy hello even as her heart pounded in her ears and she felt self-conscious, awkward and stupid.

For Bob, there was nothing significant about the meeting. His main mission in life then was to make the Harvard football team, while simultaneously helping elect his brother John to Congress. Except for his sisters, he knew few girls and he rarely knew what to say to them. Then, as throughout his life, he had no small talk.

There was the time, though, that he tried to tease Jicky Mulgrew, another of Jean's classmates. As the two girls were breakfasting at the Kennedy compound in Hyannis Port, Bob appeared with a pal, Billy Finkenstaedt, and said in a loud theatrical way:

"It's too bad there aren't any cute girls up at the Cape this summer, eh, Billy?"

"There's Betty Blackburn," Jean shot back.

Bob looked destroyed. Jean knew he had a crush on Betty Blackburn.

Jicky became a frequent visitor. Once, she could not bear Bob's groaning about a theme assignment that was plaguing him. Girls often wrote papers for boys in those days, and so, an English major at Manhattanville, she made him a deal:

"I'll write it and, if you get an A, you pay me fifteen dollars, a B ten dollars and so on."

She wrote a long discourse on the life and works of Samuel Coleridge and mailed it to Bob at Harvard. Apparently, he turned it in without reading it. Soon, he telephoned, complaining that the paper had gotten only a B.

"But, Bobby, a B is pretty good. Why are you so mad about it?"

"Well, kid, you should have seen the comments all over the paper. Everyone else did. In red ink. Comments like, 'You have a very effeminate style, Mr. Kennedy. Very flowery but interesting.'"

Jicky does not recall ever getting paid.

Ethel was hopelessly smitten with Bobby from the outset.

"He's divine," she told Jean repeatedly. "And so handsome."

But Bob remained indifferent. He showed no particular interest in Ethel, not on the ski slopes and not in Boston later, when Jean brought Ethel home with her in furtherance of her campaign to get something started between them.

Instead, Bob surprised everybody by showing up at the Skakel home on Simmons Lane in Greenwich and paying court to Ethel's sister. Pat was three years older than Ethel, at exactly Bob's age of twenty, and quieter and more serious. The family expected her to become a nun. Bob proposed marriage to her, at least once, and she gently turned him down. But he persisted, for a year and more, to the despair of her little sister Ethel.

For that lovelorn teenager, it was "that terrible period." She survived it by sheer persistence, abetted by Bob's sister Jean. Ethel managed to be around whenever Bob called for Pat, and, when Bob invited Pat to the Kennedy's Florida home in Palm Beach, Jean invited Ethel there too. Ethel outsparkled all the other girls in the athletic competitions, especially tennis, but it was still no use. Bobby remained imperturbable, out of reach, committed to Pat. But Ethel's mind was made up. All her life, it seemed to her, had been preparation for her becoming Mrs. Robert Francis Kennedy, and she was not to be denied. Here she was, bright and cheerful, a superb horsewoman and even somewhat of a tap dancer, as well as a tennis opponent to be reckoned with by all, a good and psychologically secure girl of breeding and taste—why in the world wouldn't Bob Kennedy want her for his wife? With Jean cheering her on, Ethel pressed her pursuit.

As for Pat, she continued to find Bob too immature for her liking. She drifted away and, in time, met and married an Irishman named Luan Peter Cuffe, nine years her senior and studying for a master's degree in architecture under Frank Lloyd Wright at Harvard. They moved to Dublin, where Pat acquired eight children and an Irish brogue that could lead a St. Patrick's Day parade.

And then one day Jean thought of a way to stir Bob's interest. Politics could be the road to his heart. Everybody in her family was political in one way or another, her father by appointments from President Roosevelt in commerce and diplomacy, her grandfather Fitzgerald as mayor of Boston, and now her brother John running for the Massachusetts Eleventh District seat in Congress being vacated by James Michael Curley. The fabled old "purple shamrock" was returning to Boston after two terms to resume being its mayor.

"Listen," she told Ethel, "we're all working to get my brother John elected to Congress. Bob's the campaign manager. Come on along. You'd be working with Bob."

Ethel threw herself into the 1946 congressional campaign with typical gusto. She teamed with Jean and her sister Eunice mostly, but she never missed a chance to be with Bob. Jack Kennedy won the primary and the general election and began his journey toward the White House and immortality.

But there was no immediate payoff for the Machiavellis of Manhattanville. They went back to their studies and Bobby returned to Harvard and football.

4

Bob and Ethel

*In 1950, the Korean War began. America broke relations with Commu-
nist China and fought the Chinese in Korea. The first U.S. military
advisers, thirty-five of them, arrived in South Vietnam. The year marked a
major transition for the Kennedys and their family business of politics. One
era ended with the death of John J. "Honey Fitz" Fitzgerald, Rose
Kennedy's aggressively colorful father, contemporary of James M. "Boss"
Curley and onetime mayor of Boston. The baton was passed to his grand-
son and namesake, John, who won a third term in the U.S. House and
began plotting a run for the Senate as his next step up.*

Ethel's indecision about getting married or becoming a nun
upset most of her friends too. But Dickie Mann, who later
became Mrs. Gerald Cumming, was serenely confident that
Ethel had no more than a case of prospective bride's jitters. She
could not contemplate so drastic a change in her life at so tender an age, and her natural piety drove her to consider the
alternative of a religious life. At least, that was the way Dickie
saw it.

In early 1950, Dickie popped into the Skakel residence, as she often did. There she found Ethel and her parents, George and Ann Skakel, and they were grinning at her conspiratorially. Bob was there too, and he was smiling as well.

"Well?" Dickie asked, when she could pull Ethel aside.

Ethel stuck out her left hand and waggled the fingers. A big oblong diamond sparkled there in a ring on the third finger.

And so it came to pass that, on June 17, 1950, at St. Mary's Roman Catholic Church on Greenwich Avenue in Greenwich, Connecticut, Bobby and Ethel were married in a big, traditional Catholic ceremony. John Kennedy was best man and George Skakel, a perfect picture of a father of the bride in striped pants and cutaways, gave away the white-satin-gowned bride while the church's grand organ pealed. Ethel's sister, Pat Cuffe, flew in from Ireland to be matron of honor.

Ethel's rough, tough, high-spirited brothers teamed with Bobby's Harvard football chums and his eighteen-year-old brother Teddy to comprise the cadre of ushers. Ethel's mother's eyes widened each time she saw and heard collisions in the aisle whenever any two ushers tried to occupy it or pass each other.

She inquired of the groom afterward, "Bobby, do you have any friends who weigh under 250 pounds?"

Her own tank-sized sons could have explained the situation to her in detail. They had met Bob's teammates at the bachelor dinner at the Harvard Club in New York City the night before—met, in the sense that Harvard met Yale on the football field. It all worked out all right, eventually. The Kennedys paid the club for damages.

After a honeymoon in Hawaii, the newlyweds settled into a small white cottage near the University of Virginia Law School in Charlottesville. Bob was more attentive to law studies than he had been to undergraduate work at Harvard. One reason may have been wounded pride. Virginia, in admitting him reluctantly, warned he could stay only if he did better than his "far from outstanding record at Harvard." His newfound scholarship paid off in better grades, even though his main interest was outside the classroom, revolving around the Student Legal Forum and the high-powered speakers on public issues he brought to it.

For Bob, Ethel proved the ideal mate as he embarked on this new adventure. Her gaiety and enthusiasm picked him up whenever he was down, and her ease with the social amenities filled the gaps that his own reticence occasioned.

Above all, she showered him with affection and support, and he needed that. As the seventh child and the third son, following in the wake of two acknowledged "golden boys" like Joe and John, he had never felt for very long that he belonged anywhere. That was what all his striving for personal excellence was about.

But now Ethel was there, always there, telling him that he had nothing to prove to her. She confided to Dickie Mann that she now knew that marrying Bob was the greatest thing that could ever happen to her. And she soon had Bob understanding that she loved him and admired him without limit and would always be his wife and his friend.

Bob discovered too that the only thing Ethel could do in a kitchen was wash dishes. That had been the perennial chore assigned to her by her mother, who did all the cooking without help despite the family's wealth and full complement of household retainers, and that was all Ethel ever learned to do. Her greatest triumph up to that point was a recipe for iced tea, which they brought back from their honeymoon in Hawaii.

Bob's education on this point came the hard way. Once, Ethel decided to make chicken soup for him. She took a shortcut by picking up an order from a Colonel Sanders's Kentucky Fried Chicken carryout. She dumped it into a pot of water, added parsley and salt and pepper and lit the fire. But it refused to transmogrify into chicken soup. Bob tested the result when he came home from law school and confirmed the failure.

They ate out a lot. They had friends over who could cook. And, finally, they hired a cook.

5

Settling In

Bob and Ethel Kennedy began their lives together in a time of turmoil and change. Korean War prospects brightened with the brilliant Inchon landing, and then the man who planned and executed it, General Douglas MacArthur, was fired for insubordination. Puerto Rican nationalists failed in an assassination attempt against President Truman. The people elected Dwight D. Eisenhower as the first Republican president since the 1930s Depression. The American language added two new words, "summit," describing Eisenhower's personal diplomacy meetings with his British, French and Soviet counterparts, and "McCarthyism," for the harsh inquiries of Joseph P. Kennedy's friend, Republican Senator Joseph R. McCarthy of Wisconsin, whom the Senate eventually condemned for contempt, abuse and insults.

Bob was twenty-seven and Ethel was twenty-four when they embarked on their great adventure in Washington at the outset of 1953. There was not much to set them apart from other couples of the same sort at that time. They were wealthier than most, of course, and better connected with the Washington establishment. It was thanks to those connections, largely, that they were in Washington at all: Bob's father had telephoned his friend, Joe McCarthy, and gotten him a job as assistant counsel to the Senate Government Operations Committee's Permanent Subcommittee on Investigations, of which McCarthy was the new chairman.

Bob had won wide respect and a professional status in managing his brother John's campaign for the U.S. Senate in Massachusetts that upset Republican Henry Cabot Lodge. But the cheering had hardly died down when his father gave him a typical Joseph P. Kennedy nudge.

"You haven't been elected to anything," he told Bob. "Are you going to sit on your tail and do nothing now for the rest of your life? You'd better go out and get a job."

And so, with no more of an agenda than that, Bob and Ethel returned to Washington. He had worked there briefly in 1951 and 1952, fresh out of the University of Virginia law school, as an investigator for the Department of Justice. But a call for help from Jack's floundering campaign had yanked him back to Massachusetts, where he succeeded in turning the campaign around.

In the process, though, he offended enough old-line politicians that they took to calling him "the arrogant kid" and "ruthless Robert" and the tags would stick with him for life. He never got used to it, however grimly he accepted it to deflect criticism of his brother Jack. A friendlier nickname that came later was more to his liking—"Bugs Bunny," in homage to his prominent front teeth.

It took a while for the reputation for ruthlessness to filter through to Washington however. He was promptly classified as the younger brother of the glamorous new senator he had helped elect. And he had no trouble assuming that role, telling a reporter he met at a party: "Oh, you ought to come up and see us. I've got a brother who just got elected to the Senate, and I'm on the staff of one of the committees on the Hill. Come on up and we'll talk."

But the reporter, who had seen many rich young enthusiasts take Washington jobs only to flee them for a sinecure in their fathers' businesses when they realized what a hardworking town the capital is, put that in the forget-it file. It was typical of how casually he was dismissed at first.

Bob's starting salary on the McCarthy subcommittee was $4,952.20 a year, and, despite the millions of his Kennedy inheritance (not to mention Ethel's share of the Skakel fortune), he decided to try to live within it as much as possible. He asked Ethel to go house-hunting, but he admonished, "Don't pay more than four hundred dollars a month."

With two children now—Kathleen, born on the fourth of July of 1951, just thirteen months after their marriage, and Joseph III, born September 24, 1952—it seemed likely to Bob and Ethel that they might have a large family. She was the sixth of seven children in her family, after all, and Bob was the seventh of nine. Both were devout, practicing Roman Catholics and, as Ethel put it, "we'll gladly take whatever God chooses to send us." And so, when Ethel went looking for a house with her close friend, Dickie Mann, it was with something fairly spacious in mind, and close in, to be convenient to Capitol Hill for Bob—but the rent had to be within that four hundred dollars a month limit.

The search centered primarily on Washington's Georgetown section. It had been a fairly thriving port on the Potomac River before the Founding Fathers decided to build the capital city of Washington. In the early part of this century it had become something of a slum, but the rush to Washington of Franklin D. Roosevelt's New Dealers in the 1930s had revived it. Now refurbished and chic, it had regained its almost quaint eighteenth-century look and, although prices were a little higher than elsewhere, it was where Bob and Ethel wanted to be.

Ethel and Dickie Mann searched high and low throughout Georgetown. They could find nothing that suited the young family's needs and, at the same time, fell within its budget.

Finally, their persistence paid off or, at least, in part. They found a house: 3214 S Street Northwest. It was a two-story frame cottage, with four bedrooms and good-sized living and dining rooms, plus a graceful balcony on the second floor. It was set back from the street, which ran only for one block and attracted little traffic, and was further protected by a garden and a high brick wall.

But there was a hitch: The monthly rental was more than Bob's limit.

Ethel and Dickie went to a Georgetown coffee shop to plot strategy. Should they brace Bob to raise his limit? Or would it be easier to plead for a downward revision in the rent from the owner of what Ethel and Dickie agreed was "an utterly charming little home." They decided to appeal to the owner, an army colonel who was leaving his home only because he was being transferred. They practiced their argument.

"You be the colonel," Ethel said to Dickie, and she launched into a heartrending appeal that might have been lifted from an old-time morality play. Ethel noticed, however, that as she spoke Dickie's attention wandered to the booth behind her. Dickie leaned forward and whispered, "Ethel, there's a man sitting behind you and he's an army colonel. You don't suppose . . . "

Ethel spun around and, without skipping a beat, asked the man if he owned the house on S Street. Mystified, he said that as a matter of fact he did. Ethel let out a girlish whoop and explained in a rush.

"I love your house, but I can't pay more than four hundred dollars a month rent," she said. "I was just practicing with my friend here what I was going to say to you when I called you up to beg you to let me have it for four hundred dollars."

Charmed, he agreed. And, soon afterward, the Robert F. Kennedys moved into what was really their first family home, the first of their very own. Suddenly, as it seemed, there were four children instead of two—Robert Jr. was born January 17, 1954, and David June 15, 1955—and the Bobby-and-

Ethel school of relaxed child rearing was in full swing.

David Ormsby-Gore, later to become British Ambassador to the United States on the way to becoming Lord Harlech, was struck by the simple, unsophisticated way in which the young couple lived in the house on S Street. There was no alcohol and there were no ashtrays. Raising children was the main occupation of the household, and Ethel was always bustling about, bathing and dressing and putting to bed and waking up children—in between dashing off to congressional hearing rooms, to lend moral support to whatever her husband was doing, or putting together grown-up parties for old friends and new acquaintances.

Ormsby-Gore had been a friend in England of Bob's oldest brother, Joseph Jr., a U.S. Navy pilot killed over the English Channel in World War II when the special plane he was flying, rigged as an aerial bomb, exploded prematurely, and of Bob's oldest sister, Kathleen, killed in a 1948 air crash in France. Ormsby-Gore stayed with Bob and Ethel and their brood for a week at the S Street house in 1955, and he reported:

"No doors were ever shut. Everybody wandered through every room all of the time. It was great fun. But it was quite unlike living in any other house I'd ever lived in before."

David Hackett, Bob's closest friend during prep school days at Milton Academy, was living in Montreal, Canada. But he visited them at every opportunity. He remembers the way things were then as "the happiest time—we didn't have all those worlds to conquer yet, or problems to solve."

Another frequent visitor, after he left journalism to join Bob in his investigations of labor racketeering, was Pierre Salinger. Later to be President Kennedy's press secretary, and still later a prize-winning foreign correspondent for the American Broadcasting Company, Salinger cut a somewhat erudite figure even back in the 1950s. At dinner on S Street, he was asked by Ethel what he would like to drink with his meal.

"A little red wine would be fine," he replied.

Ethel was apologetic and nonplussed. She had no wine at all, she confessed. Salinger was unruffled.

"That's all right, Mrs. Kennedy," he said. "I've got a bottle in my briefcase."

And he produced it and, in time, drained it.

The years on S Street were idyllic for Ethel, as she told her friends. She adored her husband and she gloried in whatever he was doing, cheering him on and comforting him, as the situation warranted. She delighted in the children and in the fussing with them, although she never let any of her pregnancies interfere with her extraordinarily rigorous athletic schedule. One tennis partner, an Ivy League champion while at Yale, recalled that he planned to "take it easy with her" because he estimated, as they lined up for singles, that she was about seven months pregnant.

"But then she started whizzing these balls back over the net at me, and I was suddenly in danger of physical harm," he laughed. "There was nothing for me to do but slam everything right back at her in self-defense."

For Bob, though, things were not always as he would have liked. He had plunged into his work with the McCarthy sub-committee with customary zeal. His first assignment, while McCarthy and his chief counsel, Roy Cohn, sought headlines and subversives in the State Department and the Voice of America, was to investigate Allied trade with Communist China, a combatant against Americans in Korea.

Along the way, Ethel or somebody talked him into dressing more conventionally—for example, he learned to keep his necktie pulled tight in public and even to quit wearing white sweat socks with business suits. And, for his good work, his salary was raised to $5,334.57 on April 2, 1952, and to $7,342 the following July. Still, Bob refused to give in to Ethel's argument that they needed a new car. He insisted they live within his earnings as much as possible. They continued to drive the battered, old station wagon used in Jack Kennedy's 1952 campaign for the Senate.

But he grew increasingly disenchanted with the hit-and-run tactics of McCarthy and Cohn and a young committee staffer named G. David Schine. In July, he resigned, ending six months of association with McCarthy whose taint never ceased to haunt him even though he never abandoned McCarthy, visiting with him in the grim, dark days of his fatal, wasting illness.

For Ethel and the children, the resignation was good news.

"Daddy was never home with us," one of the children remembered, "because he always seemed to be working in those days, as he would be later on too. When he quit the McCarthy committee, we thought we would have more of him, and we did, but it lasted only a short time."

Bob's father stepped into his life again. He was a member of a commission, appointed by President Eisenhower and headed by former President Herbert Hoover, then eighty years old. It was studying ways to reorganize the Executive Branch of the government. Joe Kennedy brought son Bob on as his administrative assistant.

Bob was miserable. He could not interest himself in the delicate disagreements among the geriatric set that he found himself confronting.

"They've got me looking at the Weather Bureau," he moaned.

It was, as friends noted, "a low time in his life—a time of bad doldrums." It gave him a fierce temper, a rage that he could not always keep bottled up.

Larry O'Brien, a key strategist along with Kenny O'Donnell in John Kennedy's 1952 senatorial victory and ticketed for greater glory, recalled one instance in particular. He and his wife Elva were visiting Jack and Jackie Kennedy in their Georgetown home. The Senator was on crutches, recuperating from one more back operation, a major one that he described as "the one that cures you or kills you." They went over to a Georgetown park, where Bob and Ted Kennedy were playing touch football.

Georgetown University students playing at baseball nearby

kept hitting fly balls into the game, apparently on purpose. Ted yelled at them and eventually squared off with a big fellow, about his size. But Bob broke in and pushed Ted aside, announcing he would do the fighting.

Outweighed by about thirty pounds, Bob kept punching, and so did his opponent, until it all became a bloody brawl that ended only when neither man could raise his arms any longer.

That night at Jack's house for dinner, Ethel looked at her husband's battered face and said, "Goodness! That must have been a rough game of touch."

Bob mumbled, "Yeah," and went on eating.

There were other incidents. Bob developed a habit of telling people off. Even with Ethel, when they went out in the evening, embarrassing quarrels sometimes developed. It was not a happy time at the house on S Street.

Mercifully, the spell snapped. In a reorganization of the McCarthy subcommittee's setup, the Democrats were allowed a minority counsel, and they asked Bob to take the job. He leaped at it, although in a letter to his old boss, Herbert Hoover, he commented later that McCarthy's bitter (and eventually politically suicidal) battle with the U.S. Army created partisan bickering that caused much staff tension.

"I think I shall enjoy my new job," he wrote. "However, every night when I come home from work I feel my neck to see if my head is still attached."

In short order, however, the fortunes of politics changed that. The Democrats won control of the Senate in 1954 and, with Senator John L. McClellan of Arkansas replacing McCarthy as chairman, Bob became chief counsel.

The children had more cause for complaint that he was rarely home. Whereas most congressional committees schedule three or four public hearings a year, Bob held as many as twenty-five hearings with different groups in one year of the McClellan committee's investigation of labor-management irregularities. Even traveling about the country seeking evidence, he never forgot who he was.

Carmine S. Bellino, who was Bob's prime investigator, recalled one all-night, nearly sleepless flight to Seattle that arrived at six o'clock on a Sunday morning. After checking into the Curtis Hotel, Bob hauled Bellino off to the nearest Catholic church for seven o'clock Mass.

"The church was not crowded and we sat about midway," Bellino said. "When the priest walked onto the altar, Bob saw he didn't have an altar boy. Without hesitation, he went down the aisle, jumped over the railing and served Mass."

The children had even more cause to complain about their father's absences when, under arrangements made by his father, he went with Supreme Court Justice William O. Douglas on a mountain-climbing expedition to Siberia in mid-1955. He fell ill there and when Ethel, accompanied by Bob's sisters Jean and Pat, met him September 2 in Moscow, she was aghast. She cried out to Douglas:

"What have you done to my husband?"

Back home, in the following month, fierce tragedy struck. Ethel's parents were killed in an airplane crash. She confessed to friends that she would not have found the double grief supportable except for prayer and for the strong, consistent presence of her husband at her side.

The Kennedys' cozy nest on S Street was about to disappear, literally. Their next-door neighbors, John and Catherine Warner, were divorcing and, as it turned out, she (the daughter of philanthropist Paul Mellon) gave the house to Warner (later a U.S. Senator from Virginia and for a time husband of actress Elizabeth Taylor) and bought the house on the other side of the Kennedys for herself. She then bought the Kennedys' house and, when they had been moved out, tore it down and replaced it with a swimming pool.

Bob and Ethel found another house, almost as suitable, a few blocks away in Georgetown, in the 3300 block of O Street. It was their last rental residence though, because the Greek-tragedy inevitability that seemed to shape their lives reached out for them once more.

Jackie Kennedy's loss of her first child made it unbearable for her to stay at Hickory Hill, with its new nursery that she and Jack had bought and decorated with such high hopes. She turned away from its painful reminders of what might have been.

She agreed with the rest of the family that Bob and Ethel in buying it would find it ideal for their growing family.

6

Hoffa and the Ice

President Eisenhower took no action to enforce the Supreme Court's 1954 school desegregation ruling and massive resistance to it spread throughout the South. The Soviets launched Earth's first man-made satellite, Sputnik, and the United States followed with one of its own, Explorer I. Scheduled jet airline passenger service began. Alaska and Hawaii were admitted to the union as the forty-ninth and fiftieth states, respectively. The St. Lawrence Seaway opened. Nikita S. Khrushchev toured the United States, a first for a Soviet premier. For the Kennedys, No. 1 son John won election to the Senate and, four years later, made a run at the vice presidential slot on the 1956 Democratic ticket but lost to Tennessee Senator Estes Kefauver. The family began the very next day planning a 1960 presidential bid.

Bob was one of the first guests on Jack Paar's "Tonight Show," talking about his determined efforts to jail Teamsters Union president James Hoffa. A day or two after the broadcast, Hoffa filed a libel suit against both of them for two million dollars.

Paar had never been sued before and he was worried. He called Bob and said:

"What are we going to do? We are in trouble."

Bob knew the suit was a Hoffa ploy but he could not resist.

"We certainly are in trouble," he told Paar, "if you don't have your half."

Paar saw, as others had, that Bob's hands trembled noticeably on the show, a sure sign of stage fright. Yet, Bob appeared often on "Tonight" during Paar's five-year tenure. He developed a pattern of changing into a fresh shirt in Paar's office just before going on. He would take it from a briefcase and leave the soiled shirt behind.

"I didn't want to send it back to him that way so I would take it home and my wife Miriam would wash it, as she loves to iron, and then send it on to Hickory Hill," Paar recalled. "Well, some eight years later, when I had decided to retire from television, he was concerned as to what I would do with my time. When I told him I had no plans, he suggested that I open a laundry. It took days for me to figure out what he meant."

Hoffa was no laughing matter at Hickory Hill. In their irreverent fashion, Bob and Ethel never missed a chance to wisecrack among themselves at his expense. Yet, nobody else in Bob's public life so intruded on his private life. He had set out to break Hoffa's hold on the Teamsters Union and its ties with organized crime. He knew it was too much to expect to do that without endangering the idyllic existence he and Ethel were creating at their family stronghold. He fully appreciated Hoffa's threats and the power of the *Cosa Nostra* to intimidate and avenge.

With Ethel, what concerned Bob concerned her, and she picked up on his unaccustomed alarm long before she learned its cause.

Once, in late 1962, Walter Sheridan, Bob's superb investigator, produced a "mole" in Hoffa's organization, E. G. Partin, who eventually surfaced and testified against Hoffa. When Sheridan first heard his story, he was so incredulous that he gave Partin a lie detector test, and he passed. Partin told Sheridan that Hoffa had said to him:

"I've got to do something about that sonofabitch Bobby Kennedy. He's got to go. The sonofabitch has guts. He drives around by himself in that convertible and he swims by himself in his pool. He doesn't even have any guards on his house. What do you know about plastic bombs?"

There was more. Ethel and the children, as well as various employees around Hickory Hill, noticed unusual traffic on the road out front. Big black automobiles bearing three or four burly men in tight dark suits were going by on Chain Bridge Road at a snail's pace. At least one of the men always seemed to be hanging out of a window, looking hard at the house and grounds, studying the lay of the land.

Terrifying threats came in the mail and by telephone:

"We know where your kids go to school and we know how they get there."

"Do you know what hydrochloric acid can do to your eyes?"

"Boom!"

Bob despised the very thought of bodyguards. Even when he hit the campaign trail, he had only one security man, William Barry, and he tolerated Bill because he liked him. He inveighed against bulletproof bubbletops as "those goddamned cars" and swore never to ride in one. Once, when I expressed concern about how he waded into churning crowds without protection, he told me:

"Oh, hell! You can't worry about that. Look at their faces. Those people don't want to hurt me. They just want to see me and touch me. And, if there is somebody out there who wants to get me, well, doing anything in public life today is Russian roulette."

But Hickory Hill was not in public life, as he saw it, and he was unwilling to expose Ethel and the children to the risks he took. He agreed to have U.S. marshals set up a patrol at Hickory Hill, which they did for a while off and on, first under

Chief Marshal James McShane and later under his deputy, Jack Walsh.

Throughout their long and bitter struggle, a strange truth emerged: Bob and Hoffa seemed cut from the same cloth. Bob scoffed at the notion, but many who watched their sparring believed it, and he once said it could be true only if there was a good side, where he was, and a bad side, where Hoffa was. Still, journalists stressed the similarities. Both were underdogs and backers of underdogs, prized honesty and two-way loyalty, loved their wives, worked hard and drove their staffs, spoke bluntly, abhorred dirty jokes, leaned to wry humor, courted danger and avoided tobacco and alcohol. Somebody even noticed that neither wore hats.

And they played games with each other, like jungle animals tormenting their prey. Once, on his way home after midnight, Kennedy saw lights still burning in Hoffa's nearby office. He turned around and put in two more hours at his desk. Told of this, Hoffa ordered his lights kept on after he quit every night.

Bob told Ethel about Hoffa's curious practice at hearings of fixing him with a venomous look. It was, he said, a "stare of absolute evilness" and sometimes went on for five minutes, whereupon "he would wink at me."

He was only playing a game again, Hoffa laughed years later to author Victor Lasky:

"I used to love to bug the little bastard. Whenever Bobby would get tangled up in one of his involved questions, I would wink at him. That invariably got him."

A Hoffa friend named Eddie Cheyfitz sought to bring peace by arranging a dinner meeting at his house between Kennedy and Hoffa. Kennedy suspected that Hoffa was trying to divert attention away from himself and toward Dave Beck, another Teamsters boss under suspicion. Neither Bob nor Hoffa was keen on Cheyfitz's "summit" but reluctantly agreed to it anyway.

It was February 19, 1957, and snow and ice covered Hickory Hill and everything else in the Washington area. As Bob dressed for the dinner, he joked with Ethel about what a tough guy Hoffa was and what tough guys his Mob pals were. She laughed as she buttoned up his overcoat, but her hands shook, and she said, perhaps only half in jest:

"Maybe you should be wearing a bulletproof vest."

Bob was impressed with Hoffa's firm workingman's handshake, but Hoffa thought Bob's grip was weak and condescending, about what he expected from "that rich kid." They talked some about the labor movement over dinner, although Hoffa seemed offended by Bob's direct questioning. While giving blunt and truthful answers, Hoffa kept talking about how tough he was.

"Maybe I should have worn my bulletproof vest," Bob teased. He got no response from Hoffa.

At Hickory Hill, the wait for Bob was excruciating. Ethel and nanny Ena Bernard put the children to bed and sat around and talked for a while. Ethel picked up a book. But she found it impossible to concentrate. She checked the time. It was a few minutes past nine. She went to the door and looked out.

Just then, she heard a tremendous grinding crash. On Chain Bridge Road, a car had skidded on the ice, spun around and landed in the ditch right in front of Hickory Hill. Ethel and Ena raced out and pulled the dazed driver from behind the wheel. He was terrified, babbling and shaking. They helped him up the driveway and into the house and put him, still hysterical, on the flowered chintz sofa in the little TV room. Ethel rushed to call Bob.

"I'm still alive, dear," he reassured. "If you hear a big explosion, I probably won't be."

She told him about the big explosion she had already heard. Excited herself, she described the car crash on the ice and the hysterical man on the sofa. Bob made his apologies to Cheyfitz and Hoffa and started to leave. Hoffa said:

"Tell your wife I'm not as bad as everyone thinks I am."

7

Hellzapoppin'

For America, 1960 was a year marked by college student sit-ins protesting racial segregation and by congressional passage of a strong voting
rights act, the shooting down of an American U-2 reconnaissance jet over
the Soviet Union that led to cancellation of a scheduled Eisenhower-
Khrushchev summit, and John F. Kennedy's narrow victory over Vice
President Richard M. Nixon in the presidential election.

    Suddenly, John Kennedy was the idol of the world. The first presi-
dent born in this century, he personified youth and vigor. He promised to
"get this country moving again" after the Eisenhower administration's
eight relatively quiet years. He surrounded himself with "the best and the
brightest," including his brother Robert, who accepted appointment as
Attorney General only when the president-elect said of his earlier
refusals, "This will kill Dad." Despite cries of nepotism, Robert
Kennedy survived Senate confirmation hearings. He took the helm at the
Justice Department with a key staff of overachievers—decorated war vet-
erans, Ivy Leaguers, Rhodes scholars, former Supreme Court clerks—and
committed them and himself to a grueling schedule. He brought them
home to Hickory Hill too, to work and to play there as family.

*   *   *

The great French writer André Malraux said it best, even lapsing into English, a language he almost never used.

He was on an official Washington visit as France's Minister of Culture, and Ethel, who welcomed any excuse for a party, set up a dinner in his honor at Hickory Hill. She planned it for outdoors, despite threatening weather. It was semielaborate, with a dozen or so tables under the giant oak dominating the rear of Hickory Hill. Pink, her favorite, was the theme color in the tablecloths, the candles and even the flowers.

The children were still hovering noisily, all ready for bed in colorful, mostly red pajamas and nightgowns. Some were bouncing around among early-arriving guests. Others hung from the tree or wrestled in the grass with Brumus, the huge Newfoundland, and Freckles and Megan, the cocker spaniels. And then the rains came.

"Quick, everybody," Ethel shouted. "Grab a table and get out of the rain!"

Almost at once, she realized she had no place for the tables to go. There was little space in the small dining room, and the handsome terrace later gracing the rear of the house had not yet been built. Nor had the wing for the outsized living room. Both were added in 1963, after a long campaign by Ethel for more room because of the added social burdens of having a president for a brother-in-law and a Cabinet officer for a husband.

And so, as the rains pelted down, Ethel and her guests scurried this way and that, lugging tables, looking for shelter, while the children romped and shouted and the dogs, barking and jumping, added to the fun. Mercifully, it was just a passing shower and the dinner went on as planned, eventually.

Malraux arrived in the middle of the melee. He stared. The scene reminded him of a madcap Broadway revue he had seen.

"This place is *Hellzapoppin'!*" he said.

*   *   *

And it was, most of the time. Even with a normal routine, Hickory Hill was chaotic, only semicontrolled at best. With five, six, seven, eight, nine, ten Kennedy children and assorted houseguests of all ages and interests, plus enough dogs, ponies, iguanas and what-have-yous to tax Noah's indulgence, as well as cooks, nannies and nurses either just arriving all bright-eyed and bushy-tailed or walking off the job in a huff of exhausted patience and utter frustration, and with Bob and Ethel tolerant of all the noisy hubbub and even enjoying it, what else could it be?

Nobody was safe, governesses least of all. Bob and Ethel waged a continuing struggle to keep people who would help them care for their brood. But the pace was too much. While some stayed longer than others, they all gave up in time and left, some close to hysteria. The wise, witty and even saintly Ena Bernard, who came to Hickory Hill as a nursemaid and stayed as family, was the only known survivor. Ethel became so devoted to that doughty lady that she asked her to remain, to make Hickory Hill her home, after the last of the children had grown up, and she did.

Even volunteer baby-sitters, however experienced, fell. A prime example was the case of Dotty Tubridy's mother.

Ethel and Dotty, her dear friend from Ireland, then on one of her frequent visits, had to go to the Kennedy home in Palm Beach, Florida, for a weekend social. They were to return immediately. Ena would help with the infants and toddlers, but it made no sense to take the older children along for such a quick trip. No baby-sitters could be found, a sure sign that word had spread. Up stepped Dotty Tubridy's mother.

"I'll stay here and take care of them," she said.

"Are you sure?" Ethel asked, noting Dotty's anxious expression. "I mean, you may have your hands full . . . "

"Nonsense," she snapped. "Haven't I raised ten of my own? Not to worry. I can handle them."

And so away to Palm Beach went Ethel, Dotty, Ena and the little ones, with Dotty Tubridy's mother waving them off to the airport, while standing there in the arc of the driveway at Hickory Hill. Kathleen, Joe, Bobby, David, Courtney, Michael and Kerry stood about her, looking as sweet and innocent as a choir of Botticelli angels.

That Sunday evening, Ethel called home to see how things were going.

"Everything's fine . . . now," said Dotty's mother.

Ethel jumped.

"What do you mean, 'now'?"

"Well, we were playing a game . . . "

It was one of the oldest in the book. In the game, the Kennedys talked Dotty's mother into letting them tie her to a chair in the basement. They whooped and hollered and circled her like wild savages, and she, loving mother that she was, beamed at so many lovely children at play. But, in time, she realized she had to order a halt, due to a call of nature.

"Please untie me, children," she asked sweetly.

The wild savages exchanged looks of disbelief.

"No way," they said. "You are our prisoner."

"But you must untie me. I have a special reason."

"No way," they said. "What's your special reason?"

"I have to go," she said. "You know, go."

More whoops and hollers, and a consultation.

"What should we do with our prisoner? Leave her forever? Let the wild animals eat her up?"

"Please, children, I really do have to go to the bathroom."

Another consultation, and a decision:

"Okay, but on one condition. As ransom, you have to take us to Howard Johnson's and buy us all the ice cream we want, all the flavors!"

She acceded, of course, having no choice. There is no record of her ever volunteering again to baby-sit at Hickory Hill.

*   *   *

Malraux's assessment would have been valid even at Hickory Hill parties that went off without a drop of rain. According to Ena Bernard, Ethel made her parties memorable by tying everything together into some sort of a theme.

Bob went along with whatever Ethel wanted, of course, and then threw in his own impromptu mix of guests, whether they were compatible or not—Hispanic farm activists Cesar Chavez and Dolores Huerta, for instance, along with such old-line icons as Averell Harriman and Alice Roosevelt Longworth, and athletes like Olympic decathlon champion Rafer Johnson and boxing's light heavyweight champion José Torres.

Phyllis Dillon, wife of Douglas Dillon, the former Secretary of the Treasury after whom Bob and Ethel named one of their sons, shared Malraux's assessment. Once, invited over and told to bring a swimsuit, she arrived to find the Hickory Hill pool filled with sixty orphans. She learned the same group used the pool once a week, with refreshments for all.

"It really was like running a hotel, but more difficult because no one made reservations," she commented. "Needless to say, their dining room was a bit small for such a large number of friends, but this was resolved. One time while saying grace, Ethel asked God to tell Bobby to give her a larger dining room—and Bobby did."

"This hostess with the mostest, what was her name—Perle Mesta?" Ena grinned. "Well, Mrs. Kennedy always had the mostest and *more.*"

It seemed that Ethel regarded as doomed to failure any Hickory Hill social that lacked at least one zany ingredient in the planning. She usually had three or four, like a confident chef tossing in fistfuls of oregano, thyme and basil, trusting to instinct rather than recipe. The results were hardly ever predictable.

A case in point was the Hickory Hill gathering on the Sunday after John F. Kennedy had been inaugurated as President. While waiting for him to arrive, Bob and his eldest, Kathleen, set about diverting their guests, who included Bob's old school chums, Samuel Adams and David Hackett, and one of John's old Navy pals, Paul Fay, with his wife Anita, as well as Dave's wife Judith and Kim Novak, the movie star, among others.

A half foot of snow lay on the ground and Kathleen brought out a toboggan. Soon she and Kim Novak were careening down the sloping lawn. In no time, Bob and the other men were jostling each other to get on the toboggan.

Ethel, a few yards away on skis, let out a yell of mock pique. Bob grinned and affected hurt innocence.

"Can't a father enjoy sports with his daughter?" he hollered back.

Bob hitched a pony to the toboggan and drove it around and around while the others jumped on and fell off. The pony soon tired, and Bob switched to touch football until everybody's hands became too cold to hold the ball. He brought out two horses, a gentle one for Kim Novak and a skittish one for Sam. Kim rode off gracefully on hers, but Adams's jumped sideways every time he tried to mount. In desperation, he threw himself onto the saddle and hung on until, after what seemed to him an eternity, the horse calmed down and accepted him.

Bob, watching critically but offering no assistance, smiled approval of Sam's lonely little victory, looking proud that his friend had persisted and overcome the challenge he had set him.

"Terrific!" he shouted.

The horseback riding had hardly begun when the thirty-fifth President of the United States made his entrance.

He came in standing erect on the toboggan and looking quite dignified as it rocketed down the hill. It disappeared into some snow-covered bushes and he emerged, as Sam Adams remembers, "brushing his overcoat and smiling."

At another time when snow covered the grounds, Kennedy tricks bedeviled a team of U.S. marshals assigned to Hickory Hill. The men had been sent, without fanfare, at a time when Bob and Ethel were receiving telephoned and mailed threats of harm to them and their children. Such threats were not unusual. They waxed and waned in relation to how active Bob was in pressing some public issue, such as efforts to jail James Hoffa as a labor racketeer or later to force enrollment of James Meredith as the first black student at the University of Mississippi.

Jack Walsh, the marshal heading the team, was a warm, good-hearted fellow who often saw the young Kennedy boys cooking up the devilment but generally went along with it anyway. It was, after all, a relaxant from the grim and nerve-wracking business of being constantly alert to real dangers that might or might not be out there in the dark.

Walsh found, as did Sean Rogers, my son and Bob's friend, that the Kennedy courage and fatalism and indifference to danger posed a prime obstacle. Sean, then a District of Columbia policeman on his way to becoming a lawyer, led a group of off-duty police in a similar security watch after several threats. He said:

"None of the locks on the doors seemed to work. There were no warning devices other than the dogs. What lights there were on the grounds pointed in toward the house, instead of out where the danger might be. If you were in the house and heard a noise and switched on the lights, they would blind you. Anybody out there could see you clearly in the light, but you couldn't see them."

When Walsh moved in, he got the biggest of the children's bedrooms, the one that Joe and Bobby had occupied, and they doubled up with David and Michael. As soon as his presence became familiar, however, strange things began to happen in the room.

For one thing, when he turned on the night table lamp, the bulb might explode. This had something to do with putting a penny under the bulb to cause an electricity surge. Sometimes, he would find that the wall switch did not work and, entering the room in the dark, he would become entangled in yards and yards of sewing thread strung about the room like a giant spider's web. And, of course, the simple opening of the door could mean a cascade of water from upended paper cups balanced atop it.

Outside in the snow, the Kennedy boys had a special treat for Walsh and his team, good for only one time, however. They teased the marshals into joining them in a game of tag. The air was bracing and the athletic young men, glad to stretch their limbs, accepted the challenge and raced after the boys. They chased them past the front of the house and into the large field where every summer Bob and Ethel held their charity pet show and obstacle-running contest.

Snow covered the field. It looked as level as a lake. But beneath that innocently smooth white blanket were the holes and trenches of the obstacle course, dug deeply by members of the Washington Redskins professional football team. The Kennedy boys knew where the pitfalls were. The marshals did not, until they plunged heels over head into them and came up plastered with snow.

They were victims too, of water-bagging. Anyone close to the house was subject to being targeted by a paper bag filled with water and dropped from an upper-floor window. Bob and Ethel tolerated this aerial drenching, even as occasional victims themselves, until the unthinkable happened.

They gave a dinner party for Coretta Scott King, the stately widow of Nobel Laureate Martin Luther King, Jr. A water bomb aimed her way fell just as she reached the front steps of the house. It missed. But it was the last one permitted.

Wandering into one of Ethel's parties, as Malraux did, jangled more than one set of nerves. Yet, normally staid guests might find themselves caught up in whatever wacky scheme Ethel had concocted, with Bob's connivance, and coerced into behavior that, in others or at other times, they surely would find incomprehensible.

Kenneth McCormick, the dignified editor at Doubleday who handled *Thirteen Days*, Bob's book about the Cuban missile crisis, probably never fully recovered from his experience. He was at Hickory Hill one night, working in the secretary's room with Angie Novello, Bob's secretary. She would struggle with Bob's handwriting in the final, overdue pages of the manuscript, type up what she had laboriously deciphered and hand the results to McCormick, page by page.

Suddenly, a giggling Ethel flew past the door, opened a clothes closet next to the secretary's room and got in. Angie and McCormick kept on working. Byron White, then a Justice Department lawyer and later a Supreme Court justice, came prowling around. He opened the closet and, discovering Ethel there, chuckled and got in. Secretary of Defense Robert S. McNamara came dashing by. He looked in the closet, said, "Aha!" and climbed in too. Soon, there were about fifteen men in the closet with Ethel. Angie and McCormick continued working. Finally, Bob arrived, pulled open the door, and everybody tumbled out.

McCormick was dumfounded. It was his first experience of Sardines, the after-dinner game that Ethel loved: a person hides and whoever finds that person climbs in alongside. But it was not his last experience. Within minutes, a grinning McNamara tiptoed in and hid behind the room's curtains, which, in due course, bulged with the rest of the Kennedy guests.

Angie had seen it all before. She kept on reading and transcribing, and McCormick tried to match her aplomb. But he did not fool one participant, Elizabeth Stevens, wife of movie/television producer George Stevens, Jr.

"I think he was undone by the whole thing," she observed.

Theodore White, author of *The Making of a President* and other fine books on current affairs, had a special reason to remember one Kennedy party. He was its unlikely and unwilling star.

The guests, as usual, were a motley mix, including old friend Kenneth O'Donnell, singer Harry Belafonte, Bob's sister Eunice Shriver, Georgi Bolshakov of the Soviet news agency Tass, and Charles "Chip" Bohlen, onetime U.S. Ambassador to the Soviet Union. Also as usual, barefoot Kennedy children were everywhere, dressed for bed but resisting bedtime, giggling greetings to each arrival, peeking around corners and over hedges.

White, ever the reporter, was beside himself with pleasure, and so was his wife Nancy. They went from conversation to conversation, tuning in on Belafonte's entertainer's view of Washington, applauding Eunice's pitch for her idea of a Special Olympics for retarded children, eavesdropping on Bolshakov and Bohlen, off in a corner and oblivious to the rest of the room, arguing U.S.-Soviet policy differences.

And then Bob decided to stir things up. He declared a contest to see who could do the most pushups.

He and Kenny dropped to the floor and pumped up and down for about twenty times and Bobby won. Eyes glinting, puffing from his exertions, he turned to White and said:

"Now you!"

White, small and bespectacled, was stronger than he looked, his scholarly hunch disguising muscular arms and shoulders. Delighted, he plumped himself down and wiped Bob out at, as he later recalled, "about pushup thirty-two, something like that." Pleased with himself, White looked around the room for more opponents, but there were no takers.

The bulky Bolshakov, however, challenged him to an arm wrestle and, with everybody crowded around and cheering, they began. White soon had Bolshakov's arm on the way down, and Ethel set up a yell:

"We're winning! Our side is winning! We're winning!"

Bolshakov's elbow began to lift off the table. Ethel yelled:

"You're cheating! You're cheating! He's cheating!"

Averell Harriman's seventy-fifth birthday was occasion enough for Ethel to go all out with a surprise party. She asked guests to come in costumes marking some memorable point in Harriman's long and active life.

Many appeared as railroad engineers and conductors, commemorating the Union Pacific Railroad, the Harrimans' family business. Author George Plimpton came as an Arab—Harriman had negotiated an airbase agreement with King Ibn Saud, Saudia Arabia's old "Lion of the Desert," as President Franklin D. Roosevelt's special World War II emissary. The humorist Art Buchwald dressed as a Yale coxswain, recalling Harriman's days on the Yale rowing team, and kept up a steady patter through his little megaphone, trailed by the usual coterie of dressed-for-bed children skittering about and greeting each arrival.

The proper Harriman, a man of measured merriment, was taken aback when greeted at the door by his host. Bob had on a black overcoat that touched his shoetops, with a crushed fedora riding atop his head, clothes such as those Harriman had worn as ambassador to Moscow, snitched, in fact, from his own closet.

But the pièce de résistance was yet to come. When the dinner reached the dessert stage, Ethel parted the curtains at the rear of the dining area.

Outside the bay window that overlooked the terrace there, suddenly spotlighted, appeared life-sized replicas of Roosevelt, Winston Churchill and Joseph Stalin, borrowed from the Washington Wax Museum. They were grouped as at the Yalta Conference, which Harriman had attended as an FDR aide.

There were oohs and ahs and then applause. Plimpton thought the pale waxen images "looked forlorn out there, like waifs, and awfully cold too." Somebody put a scarf around Stalin's neck and a colorful beanie on Roosevelt's head.

Bob and Ethel cooked up other simpler ways of teasing privately about the various crises he faced publicly, so as to ease their burdens and his own tensions. Once, struggling with a presidential statement on equal rights for women, they came up with this for President Kennedy to say, which, needless to mention, he never did:

"I think women should stay at home and raise children."

The Justice Department's John Doar, struggling to prevent a race riot in Jackson, Mississippi, after the assassination of civil rights activist Medgar Evers, remembers Bob demanding of him over the telephone: "How come you missed Father's Day at school?"

His top Justice aide, Nicholas DeB. Katzenbach, got a cheery send-off when he left to manage James Meredith's tumultuous enrollment as the first black student at the University of Mississippi: "If things get rough, don't worry about yourself. The President needs a moral issue."

Bob gave a surprise party for James Bennett to mark his twenty-fifth anniversary as head of the federal prison system. The cake had a file baked inside.

Yet, Bob seemed to draw a line on such jokes where children were concerned. Katzenbach recalled an incident in which a friend regaled Bob and others with a story about how his son had pilfered a cigar, smoked it and gotten violently ill. Everybody laughed but Bob, who asked, "How is he feeling?"

Bob worked incredibly hard at the Justice Department. After his brother's election, he had considered running for governor or the U.S. Senate, or perhaps seeking a university presidency. In the end, he acceded to his father's wishes and accepted appointment as Attorney General because he felt it was "the best way I can help Johnny."

To the dismay of Ethel and the children, he put in twelve- and fourteen-hour days, seven days a week. He never moved without a briefcase stuffed with things to read. He met daily with schoolchildren and young people and student groups from abroad, showing off the crayon drawings of his own children that decorated his office walls. He had a gymnasium built on the roof of the Justice Department building, and Ethel created an outdoor lunch area in the courtyard, with tables under multicolored umbrellas. He made regular tours around the Justice Department, almost invariably acting on his findings. Early on, he learned that, of the department's 955 lawyers in Washington, only ten were black, and he immediately ordered "thorough integration" of all Justice offices nationwide, and asked law schools to send him their best black graduates.

He held staff meetings constantly, digging for details, calling in attorneys who had worked at Justice for twenty years and had never been inside the office of an Attorney General, much less met one. He invited clerical and maintenance workers to the White House Judiciary receptions, previously open only to judges and the department's top officials.

But he was also a demanding taskmaster. One of his top investigative aides, Walter Sheridan, recalled an occasion when Bob ordered him to Chicago, ran into him the next morning in the office studying files on the case, and frowned, "I thought you were going to Chicago?" Sheridan explained he was booked on the noon flight and then, as he recalled:

"Bob gave me an impatient look and said, 'I never go anywhere at noon. It wastes the whole day.'

"I never went anywhere at noon again."

For Bob's secretary of thirteen years, Angie Novello, whom he called "a saint," keeping up with her peripatetic boss was often exasperating. Once, she left him a curt note saying, "It would be nice if the Attorney General, would let his office know where he is once in a while." Back came a handwritten message: "Suppose I'm lost? Love."

Angie laughed that he was indeed capable of, in effect, meeting himself coming and going. On one flight, he went from Washington to New York for a meeting and then boarded what he thought was the shuttle to Boston. At the landing announcement, he looked up from his briefcase and saw, not Boston Harbor, but the Washington Monument.

8

Touch Football

As Attorney General, Robert Kennedy struggled with major administrative problems. Not the least were differences with a nominal subordinate, Director J. Edgar Hoover of the Federal Bureau of Investigation. Hoover, an untouchable icon since the 1930s, had enjoyed a free hand for so long he countenanced no direction, least of all from a youngster born a year after he took office in 1924. But Kennedy persisted, backed by his brother the President, and, over time, forced the FBI to shift priorities from internal security—Hoover's elaborate Communist-hunting machine—to labor racketeering, organized crime and racial justice.

Yet, the fledgling Kennedy Administration's real nightmare sprang, not from the FBI, but from its sister, the Central Intelligence Agency. The CIA planned and operated the Bay of Pigs invasion of Cuba, aimed at overthrowing dictator Fidel Castro. It ended in bloody disaster, a scant three months after Inauguration Day. President Kennedy took full blame. Sobered by failure, the Kennedy brothers drew closer, gave less weight to outside advice and considered options and consequences more carefully before acting.

*   *   *

Bob's approach to football at Harvard had been that he had to work harder than his teammates because he was not as naturally equipped for the game as they were. He carried that underdog-overachiever attitude with him throughout life, in everything he did, and he pursued it in the tougher touch football games at Hickory Hill. He let up only when women and children were involved, or when he inveigled clearly outclassed friends into playing, although he pressed them if he thought they could do better by trying.

The team he assembled at the Justice Department could be said to contain a few "ringers," such as Dave Hackett, one of his closest friends who had starred at McGill University in Canada, and Dean Markham, another outstanding college player. An occasional player was Byron "Whizzer" White, brought into the 1960 campaign and the Justice Department by Bob and later elevated to the U.S. Supreme Court, a football legend irresistible to the Kennedys—All-American, Rhodes scholar, professional player.

It rankled Bob, who hated being second at anything, when Walter Sheridan, one of his top investigators, organized a team of his own that went out to Hickory Hill and beat Bob's team. Bob argued they had actually played two games that day and his side won the first, Sheridan's the other. Noting that Ethel had played, he added: "Besides, we had a girl on our team."

On a later occasion, Sheridan fought off the flu until he completed hours of delicate talks in Michigan, collapsing into bed only when they were over. The next day, he felt worse. He called Bob to say he would be out of action for twenty-four hours. Bob expressed sympathy, but added dryly: "I always say, if you're too small, don't play the game."

Bob could argue that a touch football game at Hickory Hill actually was two games or three or more, because they often lasted for hours and hours. Scores were high, and players would be going in and out of the game all afternoon. They were democratic in that Ethel or the smallest of her brood had equal status with Olympic decathlon champion Rafer Johnson, who could punt a football a country mile, or a Hall of Fame Redskin like Bobby Mitchell or Sam Huff. But they were undemocratic to the extent that Bob Kennedy always quarterbacked his side. And he seemed to favor the children, his own and others, in calling the plays.

George Plimpton first achieved fame by masquerading as a professional football player and writing about that in a splendid book, *Paper Lion*. Recalling his experiences on the Hickory Hill gridiron, he said of Bob:

"He would speak to us in the huddle: 'Now, here's what we're going to do'—he might scrabble a design in the grass for us to look at—'Bobby [Mitchell], you go down and cut to the right. Sam, same thing but you cut to the left. Rafer, go deep. That'll clear the center. David, you hold up two counts and then move to the center and I'll get the pass to you. Hang on to it."

Young David, who loved football, usually did hang on.

Plimpton commented that it was typical of Bob to have "thousands of dollars' worth of football talent deployed and decoying to allow Michael or David or Courtney to run with the ball." Any other child in the game was sure to get his number called too.

Sometimes, a touch football game would start out with dozens of people—Bob and Ethel and their dogs and children and sisters and cousins and whoever else was around—and dwindle as the day passed to a few. Anyone who wanted to play could play, with Bob in charge, and so many did that the games often looked more like street riots than games. Often, when he had the touch football going well, Bob would wander off and strike up a tennis game with his brother Ted or some other guest he knew would give him a tough game—journalist Rowland Evans perhaps, or his old school chum, David Hackett, or Gen. Maxwell D. Taylor, who was Chairman of the Joint Chiefs of Staff under President Kennedy and for whom Bob named his son Max.

U.S. marshals or Secret Service agents were on duty, they welcomed a break and, as many had college experience, they often played as hard and knowledgeably as the professionals. Long after everybody else had wandered off to eat or nap or play at something else, they were were still banging away in the failing light.

Jacqueline Kennedy never did get the hang of it. For her husband Jack's sake she tried for a while, but she was doomed from the moment she asked, "If I get the ball, which way do I run?" She preferred the sidelines, a comfortable lawn chair and a good book.

Once, when Jack made a spectacular catch, he danced past her, saying, "Hey, Jackie, did you see that?" She barely looked up, absorbed in her book. Bob wandered over and said softly, "It would help if you could say something nice. It would mean a lot to him." She put the book down and worked at cheerleading after that.

If the game was not touch football, it was racing in the pool or horseback riding or tennis or anything else that was a test. At Hyannis Port, it was sailing and sailing races and swimming in cold choppy water miles from shore. Out west, it was skiing and climbing and hiking and riding the rapids. Bob and Ethel, equally competitive and united in their love for each other and adventure, were rearing their children to follow their example—dare to try, play to win, no excuses when you lose, no flinching from pain or danger, no complaints ever. And, on those terms, their friends and fellow workers were welcomed into the fold.

Thomas Corcoran, an Olympic skier who hosted Bob and Ethel often at his ski resort in Waterville Valley, New Hampshire, watched Bob progress from indifferent to excellent on the slopes. He saw Bob try a slalom course three times before he made it and then, instead of stopping, keep on the trail, miraculously clearing rocks and tree roots safe only for walking.

Corcoran summed up what Bob sought in sports this way:

"To be outdoors and away from the cities in the winter meant mountains; in the summer, it meant water. He sailed with the same intensity that he skied: with skill and abandon, confidence and determination. He obviously enjoyed approaching the brink of the impossible. In a man who appreciated good judgment in others, he seemed in sports to be testing his own assessment of risks, whether it was floating on an air mattress into the roar of rapids he had not seen, or sailing at night or in storms. To be outdoors was a chance to be with his children, Ethel and, usually, some friends. It was also a chance to test his will, daring and ability against the forces of nature."

Willy Schaeffler, a veteran of the German Army in World War II, once laughed that surviving the retreat from Moscow, as he had, was easier than running Christmas ski races at Aspen, Colorado, and Sun Valley, Idaho, for forty-six assorted Kennedys and friends. Schaeffler was struck by the zest and abandon with which Bob skied. He particularly remembered one occasion on which he warned Bob not to go too fast on deep, fresh snow:

"Of course, Bob ignored my warning. He went much too fast, and spilled. Ethel and I saw him tossed high into the air. I heard Ethel cry out, 'Oh, God!' Then Bob disappeared. He was swallowed by a big snow hole. Would he be hurt? I raced down to the rescue, followed by the others.

"There he was, smack in the middle of a soft snow circle, surrounded by jagged rocks. His ski bindings were torn to pieces. His skis were broken. And, in the fall, he must have brushed one of the rocks, for he was bleeding from a facial wound. And laughing.

"That seemed typical of him. His raw guts, and the ability to test himself and to accept the consequences."

James Whittaker, conqueror of Mount Everest and Bob's guide and companion when they became the first to climb the Yukon's Mount Kennedy, named for his brother Jack, had misgivings when he first met him. Whittaker thought he looked too fragile to make the climb. His suspicions were reinforced when Bob told him the last thing his mother said to him was, "Don't slip." And, when he asked Bob what he had been doing to get in shape, the reply really worried him:

"Running up and down the stairs at home and practicing hollering, 'Help!'"

After their successful climb, Whittaker went with Bob to Hickory Hill to meet Ethel and the children. There, Whittaker recalled, "I learned how he kept in shape." His summation:

"I stayed with the family five days and almost required the help of a stewardess to board the plane at National. I was so stiff and bruised from touch football, tennis and just running around (I lost at that too) that I headed for the mountains to restore my damaged ego, and I began to wonder what there was that Bob could not do. . . .

"There is not any mountain he could not have climbed."

One thing that Bob did not do, although he planned to some day, was fight a bull. On a South American tour, he met Manuel Benítez Pérez, the renowned Spanish matador known as El Cordobés, in Lima, Peru. They posed for a picture grinning, arms about each other, looking like schoolboys. It appeared in the paper the next day captioned, "The two most famous hair bangs of the century *mano a mano*"—literally hand to hand, describing a *corrida* in which two matadors alternate competing fighting bulls.

They became fast friends and kept in touch. At their last meeting, in Caracas, Venezuela, Bob laughingly challenged El Cordobés to a *mano a mano* "when I come to Spain and visit you in Córdoba."

He never made the visit, but some years afterward his son Joseph, later a U.S. Congressman from Massachusetts, did as a teenager. He fought one of the bulls on El Cordobés' ranch and wound up gored, although not seriously.

Bob would have loved it. He too had been a reckless, awkward teenager, and he often saw himself in young Joe.

Kay Evans, wife of journalist Rowland Evans and a classmate of Ethel's at Manhattanville, survived four summer cruises in a row with Bob and Ethel up the coast of Maine. These were as unorthodox as anything else that Bob and Ethel undertook—fourteen people squeezed into a boat meant for six, with Bob the only one a qualified sailor, no navigators, road maps for sailing charts, meager provisions, children, Freckles the cocker spaniel and, of course, enormous trust in the Lord. Kay Evans said that, except when Bob steered, their usual state was "lost lost lost."

Dean Markham, a fine football player but no seaman, at the helm one night was asked what course he was on. He replied:

"Slightly to the left of the moon."

George Stevens, the movie and television producer, starred on one trip, his first ever. He went below when things were quiet and came up in full costume as an eighteenth-century admiral—gold braid, flouncy epaulets, huge Captain Bligh hat and all. As it happened, Michael Forrestal, an old friend and a serious sailor, came along about that time and, spotting the Kennedy yawl through the mists, saw what he took to be "a circus on board."

"There were not only a great many people on the boat, some in costume, but also a menagerie of animals," he reported later. "We came alongside . . . and found Bobby in the bow, standing outboard of the genoa, really looking as if he wanted to have nothing to do with this turmoil that was going on on the deck behind him."

On another trip off Maine, headed from Portland to Campobello, Bob and Rowland Evans were taking the sun on the foredeck, reading and talking. The air was warm but the water was cold, below fifty degrees. Bob laid aside his prize, the leather flying jacket with presidential seal given his brother Jack aboard the nuclear carrier *USS Enterprise*.

A sudden gust of wind lifted it off the deck and into the

water. Bob kicked off his canvas shoes and plunged over the side. He caught up with the jacket about a hundred yards astern and, after about four minutes of bobbing in the choppy seas, he was pulled back aboard, shivering, lips purple, teeth chattering. It was said that twelve minutes was the limit of survival in such water.

"I thought at the time, and I still think, that I have never known anyone with courage enough to dive into such dangerous waters without hesitation or fear," Evans commented later. "There was just one thing for Bobby to think about, one thing to be done. He had to get his brother's jacket. There was no luxury of choice. He went."

A couple of years later, he had to do it again. Standing on the rear of a sloop moored at Deer Isle, he looked into the water and saw his dog Freckles there, struggling for his life. He jumped in fully clothed and pulled him out.

Another memorable cruise was a weekender that Bob and Ethel took in late September 1965 with all available children, dogs and friends. They broke off from Washington duties, flew up to Hyannis Port and, amid the usual chaos of clothes and duffle bags and shouting and singing, set out for Newport to visit Senator Claiborne Pell of Rhode Island. A chilly squall blew up and, with outdated charts in unfamiliar waters, as usual, they struggled into harbor well after dark, for hot tubs, supper and sleep at Pell's house.

The next day, they left about noon for the return to Hyannis Port. The weather had gotten worse. There were no other boats in sight. Tossed by thirty-mile-an-hour winds on heaving waves, some fifteen feet high, adults as well as children were subdued from the day before. They lunched quietly on peanut butter sandwiches and put their trust in Bob's seamanship.

Suddenly, they were startled by the sound off in the distance of a siren wailing somewhere, and then they saw a U.S. Coast Guard cutter closing in on them at high speed.

E. Barrett Prettyman, who had been a Justice Department

lawyer and was along on the two-day trip, remembered thinking they probably were going to get reprimanded for being out in such dangerous weather. Somebody joked:

"What are they going to do, tell us to pull over to the curb?"

But the message that came over the bouncing cutter's bullhorn, in a deep voice heard through the howl of the wind, was no joke:

"Mister Kennedy, your daughter Kathleen has been injured by a horse and has head and internal injuries. But the doctors say she is all right. Do not be concerned. Pull your mainsail and we will try to come close enough to reach you."

Ethel turned ashen and dropped her head. She looked about like a trapped animal, seeming in an instant to recognize their grim situation. She wanted to go to Kathleen, and she wanted Bob to go with her, but it was clear one of them would have to stay with the children on the boat. And, then too, how could either of them transfer to the Coast Guard cutter in such wild seas?

"Give me a minute," Bob said. He sat steering the boat, staring straight ahead, not speaking. He knew he would lose control if he lowered the mainsail, and the two vessels would crash if the cutter came alongside to take him aboard. He stood up, signaled the charter captain to take the helm, said goodbye to Ethel and the children and went over the side.

"We all held our breath," Prettyman reported later. "He bobbed about in the waves, fighting desperately to stay on top. The cutter maneuvered quickly behind us, and he was somehow able to reach its ladder. They pulled him aboard, and we all sighed in unison."

The cutter raced off with a roar. It crashed through the towering waves with such force that Bob's chair, next to the helm, broke apart and he sprawled on the deck. Just then, the cutter's front window shattered and showered glass all around the cabin.

Bob had barely reached shore when Ethel received a radio

message that Kathleen was fine, her condition not really serious. Ethel knew Bob too well not to see through this too-quick reassurance. Her anxieties began to ease after a second Coast Guard cutter arrived and guided the boat to shore. They ended after she was flown to Kathleen and saw for herself that she was, by then, really all right.

Melody Miller, a press aide to Bob and later to his brother, Senator Edward M. Kennedy, recalled weekends of strenuous sports at Hickory Hill, hosted by Bob and Ethel. They were great antidotes for the normal tensions created by hard work at the office. But most staffers, she recalled, limped in bruised and battered and nursing sore muscles on Monday.

"Our minds were eased but our bodies were wrecked," she laughed. "Yet, it was wonderful for everybody. Touch football, races in the pool, footraces across the lawn, sitting around talking—a wonderful picnic atmosphere. Imagine, there we were, going out for a pass thrown by a Walter Sheridan or talking football tactics with a Washington Redskin or exploring the art of speechwriting with a Ted Sorensen. It was terrific, especially for the young interns."

José Torres had a special recollection too. As light heavyweight champion of the world, the gentle boxer had become the idol of fellow Puerto Rican immigrants in New York. He had guided Bob through upper Manhattan's El Barrio and helped him understand the special problems there, when Bob ran for U.S. Senator from New York, and after he won. Bob occasionally brought Torres home with him, delighting the children.

Torres remembered a time at Hyannis Port when Bob rousted him after only a few hours of sleep and dragged him downstairs to have breakfast with "an army of kids"—all freckle-faced, all yelling, all laughing, all Kennedys. After eating, he tried to slip back upstairs for more sleep, but Ethel handed him sneakers, shorts and a T-shirt, and announced, "Tennis."

After tennis, he was hauled off for a couple of hours of sailing and swimming some five miles at sea. Ashore again, he tried to go upstairs to finish sleeping. He was intercepted by David Kennedy, then about twelve, coming across the lawn with boxing gloves.

Torres refereed Kennedy youngsters pounding each other in good-natured glee, and it was all great fun for a while. Then somebody said:

"Box Daddy, José! Box Daddy!"

David appointed himself Torres's cornerman and whispered as he laced the gloves on:

"Knock him out in the first round so he won't suffer."

Some of David's brothers and sisters and cousins were not so merciful. Jumping around the imaginary ring, they shouted to José:

"Hit him in the head!"

"Hit him in the belly!"

"Let him go eight rounds and *then* knock him out!"

Torres danced about, dodging and sidestepping but not punching. Try as he might, Bob could not hit him.

"Let me knock you down," Bob whispered. José nodded. Bob threw a wild punch and Torres went down motionless on the wet grass. Bob hopped around him, arms raised high in triumph, yelling at the top of his lungs:

"Get a camera, somebody! Please, get a camera!"

Torres, his eyes closed tight, started giggling.

"Don't laugh," Bob said. "You'll spoil it."

9

The Pool

President Kennedy pushed America's come-from-behind effort in the space race with the Soviet Union. The first communications satellite was launched. Alan B. Shepard, Jr., made the first U.S. suborbital space flight, and John H. Glenn, Jr., circled Earth three times as the first American in orbit. Glenn, shy and self-effacing, became a frequent guest at Hickory Hill, another hero collected and brought home by Bob Kennedy as family.

People were pushing people into swimming pools long before Bob and Ethel Kennedy built theirs. It became a great American pastime soon after Thomas Alva Edison created the first backyard pool for his summer home in Fort Myers, Florida, at the turn of the century. But, in the early 1960s, the nation was beguiled by the Kennedy mystique and its accent on youth and vigor, and it followed the goings-on at Hickory Hill as avidly as the antics of Hollywood celebrities. The Olympic-sized swimming pool, with its big, graceful cabana as a backdrop, soon became a centerpiece.

The pool, and throwing people into it, was a symbol of a robustness that Washington had not known since the presidency of Theodore Roosevelt. Hickory Hill seemed to those visiting it, and the journalists reporting on it, to be crawling with children at all times, not all of them Kennedys. Bob might come home unannounced, trailing forty or fifty inner-city kids and leading them into the pool, with hamburgers afterward for all around. Or he might show up with a coterie of his office staffers and their children.

With so many of their own that Ethel kept a filing-card system on them—recording dental visits and measles dates and the like, plus how they were doing in school and other pertinent data—the days around the pool were like some early Disneyland. Bob and Ethel pushed their dedication to physical fitness and high spirits there, on the tennis court, in touch football across the sloping lawn, and in horseback riding on backroads and woodland trails. Even while doing all that, they were planning skiing, hiking, sailing and river-rafting for other places and other climes.

Once, the ghost of Edison contemporary Teddy Roosevelt reached out to put Bob's grit to a severe test. President Kennedy had found a 1908 letter in which the old Rough Rider declared that Marines should be fit enough to hike fifty miles in twenty hours. He sent it over to Marine Commandant David Shoup, a World War II Medal of Honor winner, asking whether his Marines could do that and pledging, in turn, to check out the White House staff. That sent White House press secretary Pierre Salinger and just about everybody else running for cover. But Bob at the Justice Department decided to take up Shoup's inevitable challenge to join the Marines for the hike. He did it, along the Chesapeake & Ohio Canal from Washington to Camp David, Maryland, slogging painfully to the finish.

An overlooked irony, perhaps, is that Edison, the original pool man, detested exercise. He built his pool, he said, for his children and his guests. He said: "God gave us the human body just to carry our brain around and we only use about one-tenth of our brain, so why exercise the body?" He lived to be eighty-four.

Like any other suburban hostess of means, Ethel planned her warm weather parties around the pool. The big difference was that hers almost always involved huge numbers of guests, many of them household names in government and sports and entertainment, although some had never laid eyes on each other before. Ethel was an expansive party-giver, and Bob, as his old Harvard classmate Kenneth O'Donnell once said, "kept making close, personal friends all of his life."

At a party for John Glenn, the astronaut who later became a U.S. Senator from Ohio, the theme-conscious Ethel decided to honor him with an approximation of the vast, dangerous outer reaches of space. The pool was the closest simulation available. She set up a precarious catwalk across it, with a table for two at the center. The idea was that she and Glenn were to have their dinner there while all the other guests dined around and about poolside.

But Glenn, for all his derring-do as a Marine combat pilot, a test pilot and the first American in orbit, held back. He managed to maneuver adroitly away from the pool and never joined Ethel on the shaky board. His reaction, in fact, was to scribble a note on a paper napkin—"Help! I'm a prisoner at the Kennedys!"—and send it aloft attached to a party balloon. It was borne quickly on the wind across the trees and never seen again.

Ethel was having a huge time at pool center, laughing and coaxing, but failing to lure Glenn or anybody else out to her swaying perch. Arthur Schlesinger, Jr., long a Kennedy adviser and later biographer, was in proper academic attire, dark suit and trademark bow tie, the most sedate of guests. He claimed afterward that he saw Ethel's chair slipping and went to the edge of the pool, thinking he might somehow prevent her from falling in. When she did tumble, he said, he stood pondering whether to go in after her and help fish her out.

The decision was made for him. Lee Udall, wife of the

Kennedy administration's Secretary of the Interior Stewart Udall, took a running head start and gave Schlesinger a mighty shove that sent him flying almost to the center of the pool. Alice Roosevelt Longworth, the venerable daughter of Theodore Roosevelt, was among the guests and an eyewitness.

She was no stranger to high jinks in high places. Then a beautiful, stately old lady, she had been a rather obstreperous teenager when her father was President. She inspired the delightful and ageless song, "Alice Blue Gown." In his inauguration parade, he had her ride with him, perhaps to his regret. She kept hanging out of the carriage, waving and cheering back at the people, enormously exhilarated. Finally, Teddy tugged her back inside, scolding, "Alice, this is my inauguration, not yours."

At the Kennedy pool, she noted with great amusement how Glenn managed to stay away from Ethel. She quietly approved of his prudence. And then:

"I shall never forget. . . Suddenly, practically over my shoulder, shot Arthur Schlesinger. He claims that he doesn't know whether he was pushed, or whether he jumped, or what happened. He says he doesn't remember, but he gave the impression of being catapulted."

Said George Plimpton, another eyewitness: "He was very indignant."

Schlesinger eventually conquered his indignation and forgave Lee Udall. But he never convinced Ethel, nor Alice Roosevelt Longworth, that, with or without help, he would have wound up in the pool that night.

10

The Academy

Vietnam fighting was developing a vortex, drawing in the United States as it had the French before. President Kennedy authorized the handful of U.S. military advisers there to fire back if fired upon. Attorney General Robert Kennedy, as his brother's closest confidant in all matters, worked closely with the Pentagon and the State Department in coordinating, if not actually directing, the burgeoning U.S. commitment.

Another commitment was taking hold in the South. Emboldened by the liberal, call-to-action tone of President Kennedy's inaugural address, James Meredith applied for admission the next day as the first black student at the University of Mississippi. Robert Kennedy's assistant for civil rights, Burke Marshall, became a frequent visitor to Hickory Hill, working long after-hours and occasionally being coaxed into family games. More intellectual than athletic, he preferred the mind games. The civil rights pot was boiling in the South and Marshall and the Kennedys would soon have to handle it.

Bobby Kennedy's zest for sports and physical adventures that tested his mettle had its counterpart in the quieter precincts of the mind. He had admittedly been a poor student as a boy and at Harvard. But, somewhere along the line, a spark ignited and he was off in pursuit of learning with the same high-spirited dedication he brought to skiing and mountain-climbing. Suddenly, it seemed, he had embraced Juvenal's *mens sana in corpore sano*—a sound mind in a sound body—and he had books everywhere, serious works that trained and uplifted, and he became as quick as his brother Jack at memorizing aphorisms and poetry.

The awakening may have begun on his grand tour of Europe and the Middle East following graduation from Harvard in 1948. He returned shaken by the human misery he saw and more determined than ever to "make a contribution." Even more, he began to see things in shades of gray instead of black and white.

Bob's intellectual growth, as the years passed, was a virtual secret amid the glare of publicity surrounding Kennedy touch football, skiing, sailing, tennis and the like. But it was there to see, a source of wonder among family and friends. He could amaze with a sudden apt quotation, gentle or biting and usually self-deprecating. For miscreant children, there were no physical blows, except maybe a passing swat across the seat. But there was the dreaded "look," a paternal scowl of disappointment that could wound, and assignments to memorize and recite wholesome poetry.

There were always contests of reading and reciting at the dinner table, and even singing, although Bob's voice reminded some of fingernails drawn across a blackboard. His best number was "Jingle Bells." At the table, he and Ethel always made a great fuss over exceptional performances. Kathleen and Joe, the oldest, recalled the time he pitted them against each other in a contest of speed-memorizing some lines from Tennyson. They finished in a dead heat and he gave them both first prize.

In all this, Ethel backed him up with a gaiety and enthusiasm that was so infectious it never failed to send the children into rollicking laughter. Their self-fulfillment was in pleasing their father and hers was in helping to make that happen for them all.

As to Bob's own capacity for consuming words, Arthur Schlesinger, Jr., the Kennedys' resident intellectual and biographer, recorded that, between Christmas of 1962 and Easter of 1963, Bob read E. S. Creasy's *Fifteen Decisive Battles of the World*, S. F. Bemis's *John Quincy Adams and the Foundations of American Foreign Policy*, Irving Stone's *They Also Ran*, Alan Moorhead's *The White Nile*, Barbara Ward's *The Rich Nations and the Poor Nations*, Herbert Agar's *The Price of Union*, Barbara Tuchman's *The Guns of August*, Cecil Woodham-Smith's *The Great Hunger*, Paul Horgan's *The Conquistadors in North American History* and Fletcher Knebel and Charles Bailey's *Seven Days in May*.

It was to Schlesinger that Bob turned with an idea that he and Ethel cooked up after attending a summer seminar in Aspen, Colorado. Why not, they said, create a similar set of seminars at Hickory Hill? Why not invite the best brains in America to come before the Kennedys and their guests and expound on their specialities, much as Bob had done with the Student Legal Forum in Charlottesville? Shouldn't high-ranking members of the Kennedy administration be exposed to great ideas outside the government, outside their own tight little orbits?

To the quiet and thoughtful, if occasionally acerbic, Schlesinger, the idea seemed half-baked. He had been to a few of Ethel's theme parties at Hickory Hill and did not relish the distinction of being the first pushed into the swimming pool. This sounded to him like another theme party in the making. He tried to forget about it and hoped Bob and Ethel would too.

No such luck. Ethel had few intellectual pretensions and little curiosity about the arcane mysteries of nuclear fission and such. But she had seen how the Aspen seminars excited Bob, and what he wanted she wanted. She kept the idea alive, reinforcing Bob's pressure on Schlesinger with sly little teasing reminders at every turn. The first seminar met on November 17, 1961, and Hickory Hill Academy was born.

Not all of the sessions were held at Hickory Hill, although Bob was in charge of the format and guest list as the organizer and ringleader. A traveling circus, it went from house to house. The speaker would talk for about forty minutes and the Cabinet officers, Supreme Court justices and whoever else the Kennedys had invited would fire questions and then take the floor with views of their own. They, in turn, would have to defend their statements against the others. Sometimes, as many as sixty people, including some spouses, would be crowded into Ethel's spacious sitting room or wherever, chafing at the bit to have a say.

"There was nothing precious about these lectures," Alice Roosevelt Longworth recalled. "It was all sorts of fun, that was all. Fun to watch all the people who were there."

Among the funniest lecturers at Hickory Hill Academy was Al Capp, the creator of the comic strip *Li'l Abner*. The biggest bore, as far as Ethel was concerned, was Mortimer Adler, the educator famous for his espousal of "The Hundred Great Books."

"Dr. Adler talked and talked and talked," Ethel said. "He wouldn't give anybody else a chance to say anything. And I had Father Francis Cavanaugh of Notre Dame there with us. I wanted to hear him speak too."

One night, at Averell Harriman's home in Washington's Georgetown, the lecturer was Dr. Lawrence S. Kubie, a well-known psychiatrist. His subject was "Urban Problems and Poverty Children." Bob challenged Kubie on whether America had time to psychoanalyze the ghetto when immediate action was needed to cure its ills. Somebody broke in to demand what made the ghetto's psychological problems any different from those of the affluent.

That sent Kubie into a long story about how he had spent a summer vacation on the most isolated island he could find, off the coast of Alaska. Alice Roosevelt Longworth remembered well what happened next to Secretary of the Interior Stewart Udall:

"And Udall went to sleep—that was at Averell Harriman's. He went to sleep, and they woke him up. He went to sleep again . . . Udall just went to sleep. Bored, probably. He went to sleep and he snored a lot. . . . Then he was awakened. We always laughed about it. He was awakened, yes, and he went back to sleep again."

The story Udall slept through was one of Kubie's favorites: On his first day on the isolated island, he went out with a local fisherman who asked what kind of doctor he was. Upon learning Kubie was a psychoanalyst, he poured out his troubles. The next day, practically every fisherman on the island lined up on the dock to take him out. When his vacation ended, Kubie said he knew all the islanders' fears, frustrations, hopes and so forth. And he said they were the same as those he heard in his Baltimore office.

At that point, Ethel spoke up: "Dr. Kubie, how would you like to spend your vacation at Hyannis Port this summer?"

John Kenneth Galbraith, the well-known economist who was then U.S. Ambassador to India, came home for consultations and wound up lecturing at Hickory Hill Academy. He drew a large crowd at Supreme Court Justice Potter Stewart's house. It included, besides Bob and Ethel, such Kennedy administration stalwarts as Secretary of Labor Arthur Goldberg, economist Walter Heller and national security adviser Walt Rostow, with their wives. The prickly Galbraith provoked Heller into a heated debate by accusing the New Frontier of shortsighted failure to provide enough funds for welfare, the cities and the arts. Goldberg jumped in on Galbraith's side and Rostow tried to reconcile differences.

"Bobby confined his role to interrogation," Galbraith remembered. "But he was a very rapt and eager prosecutor of the positions. You had the feeling that, if you were shabby on any important point, you could pretty well count on

Bobby to come in and press you on it. This was matched in some degree by the eagerness of the questioning that Ethel put.

"It stands in my mind as a bright, lively and professional evening."

11

Brumus

James Meredith's enrollment as the first black student at the University of Mississippi touched off a riot that took three thousand U.S. troops to put down. One man, a French journalist, was killed, and other persons were injured. The Kennedy administration met with Dr. Martin Luther King, Jr., and other black activists, but failed to convince them of its sincerity in protecting the rights of minorities. Rachel Carson published her book, Silent Spring, *launching the environmental movement. The Supreme Court declared laws requiring prayer in public schools to be unconstitutional. Increasingly the President's closest adviser, Robert Kennedy grew as a public figure, attracting many critics, detested by conservatives, distrusted by liberals. He found solace at Hickory Hill, with his children and their pets.*

Was there ever another dog like Brumus? It was not possible to look at him without an urge to laugh. He had clown written all over him. But he also had a talent for wearing out his welcome in a hurry, and in a way that was no laughing matter. He was a big shaggy mountain of an immovable object at rest and an irresistible force on the move, gregarious but snappish in any social situation, with bad breath, an ability to drool at will—picking his targets among the more fastidious and the least dog-indulgent—and with a pompadour that hid his eyes. His odoriferous coat was flat black, having no sheen at all anywhere, except for the patent leather nose and lolling tongue, red as a raspberry. He was one enormous ink spot when collapsed, which was most of the time, and a blob of fuzzy soot when up and about. When he slowly sashayed across the lawn, head down and laboring in the effort of movement, he gave the impression of being some giant, prehistoric, furry black caterpillar. He looked as if he had been drawn by James Thurber and colored by Hermann Rorschach. He was, in reality, a gift to Bob and Ethel from Thurber, the godfather of all Newfoundlands whose drawings immortalized the breed, although the Kennedys never determined whether the puckish humorist meant it as a joke or not. And, as for the psychiatrist Rorschach, Brumus provoked as wide a variety of judgments as any of those famous tests.

"What's the matter, don't you like friendly dogs?" Bob asked a friend in mock seriousness at Hickory Hill one day, as she cringed from Brumus, who was maneuvering around as if to jump into her lap.

"Dogs, yes," she said through gritted teeth. "Ponies, no."

He was not much of a success as a pony, either, as he and the whole family found out at a horse show. It was an important show for the girls, Kathleen and Kerry, who were both in it. So was their cousin Caroline, whose mother was also there giving support, along with Bob and Ethel and every other Kennedy not away at school or otherwise unavailable, plus close friends like LaDonna Harris, wife of Oklahoma Senator Fred Harris.

Unfortunately, Bob insisted on bringing Brumus too. And, when everybody was preoccupied with applauding and urging on the girls, Brumus left the stands and sat in the middle of the ring. The master of the show, thus impaired, looked flustered, according to LaDonna Harris.

"Would somebody kindly get their dog out of here?" he begged. "The dog is disturbing the horses."

With that, he gently nudged Brumus with his foot.

Bob was out of the stands like a shot.

"Don't kick my dog," he said, cold and hard.

The poor man floundered even more.

"Sir, I didn't kick your. . . "

"I saw you!" Bob said in the same brittle way. "Don't you ever kick my dog again."

He led Brumus from the ring.

"Oh, my gosh!" Jacqueline Kennedy groaned. "We're going to lose the horse show."

Even at Hickory Hill, at Bob and Ethel's annual pet shows to benefit Washington's Northwest Settlement House for underprivileged children, Brumus could be counted on for a major gaffe, sooner or later. If he was not trying to eat the small pets or snap at a strange child, it would be something else. The Kennedy consensus was to lock him up for the day, and a large pen was built for that purpose, but Bob would not hear of it when he was around.

Brumus achieved Hall of Fame status for gaucherie at the very first pet show. Bob was sitting on the lawn, petting him, when Brumus suddenly pulled himself up and wandered away. He went over to two women who were lounging on the lawn, quietly having their lunch, and he lifted his leg and wet them down, almost ceremonially. Bob blanched and ran into the house. Brumus was then exiled there with him but escaped. He ambled over to the same two women, by then watching children riding the carousels, and did it again.

The humorist Art Buchwald, seeing it all, chided Bob for his disappearing act. He said it hardly met the ideals espoused by his brother Jack in his Pulitzer Prize book, *Profiles in Courage.*

Buchwald was chief judge and master of ceremonies at the pet shows. He awarded prizes on the basis of which pet had the longest nose, the crookedest tail, the nicest smile, the oddest color and so on. Journalists Rowland Evans and Philip Geyelin, among others, helped with the judging. Often, because there were so many of them, a Kennedy or Kennedy kin would mostly win. Sometimes, as happened with Willy Smith, son of Bob's sister Jean and then about seven, Buchwald's decisions were protested.

Buchwald and his wife, Ann, were dining with Ethel, the Smiths and other friends and family one night when Willy came in carrying his pet chameleon. He sibilated through missing front teeth that he should have won first prize instead of second, and he put the little creature on the table. Five inches long, slate gray, looking like a miniature dinosaur carved from marble, it suddenly moved. An astonished Ann Buchwald reported:

"It walked between the soup plates and over to the flowers."

Buchwald declared:

"Oh, it *walks*! I didn't know it walked! *Of course*, it gets first prize."

When he got home, Buchwald took one of the blue first-prize ribbons left over from the show, put it in an envelope with a formal letter of apology and sent it to Willy.

Buchwald proved an irresistible target for Brumus eventually. In the midst of a spiel at the 1967 show, he found himself under siege. Rescued by a rush of all Kennedys within sound of his yells, Buchwald decided, nevertheless, to stir things up further. He had Edward Bennett Williams, the renowned criminal lawyer, take the "case."

Williams's friendship with the Kennedys was back on track after being chilled when he defended Jimmy Hoffa against Bob's efforts to put him in jail. Williams used his best lawyer's stationery and legalistic style in a letter to Bob:

"I have been retained by Mr. Art Buchwald to represent him in the matter of the vicious and unprovoked attack made on him Wednesday, July 25, by the large, savage, man-eating, coat-tearing black animal owned by you and responding to the name, Broomass (phonetic).

"Mr. Buchwald has been ordered to take a complete rest by

his physician until such time as he recovers from the traumatic neurosis from which he is suffering as a result of the attack. He will be in isolation at Vineyard Haven, Martha's Vineyard, Massachusetts, for an indefinite period at a cost of $2,000 a month."

Bob and Ethel were not above using Brumus as a foil. Once, Bob and Rowland Evans got into a political argument at dinner. The next night, Rowly and his wife Kay were just sitting down to a small dinner party of their own when Bob and Ethel arrived—"uninvited, unannounced and unexpected," as Kay put it, but grinning broadly.

With them was Brumus, to add a homey touch and to show there were no hard feelings.

Why was Bob Kennedy so protective of such an oaf? Was it, perhaps, because as the underdog of underdogs he touched that tender spot inside Bob that always responded to the disadvantaged, especially the friendless? With so little to recommend Brumus, it was natural that Bob should rally to his side. He willingly suffered the loss of social acceptance, even all the grumbling, for that. And Brumus repaid him the only way he knew how, by following him about as if on a string.

Few of Bob's friends and coworkers were cut from the same St. Francis of Assisi cloth. Bob's secretary, Angie Novello asked him once why he brought Brumus at times to the office, inconveniencing staffers who did not share his love of dogs.

"Well, if he sees me leaving the house in the morning, he just whines and cries, and I just can't stand it."

Angie recalled one occasion when she was ushering a foreign diplomat into the Attorney General's office. Brumus had taken up a position in the doorway, making it impossible to enter without leaping over his great bulk.

"General, here is the ambassador," Angie announced, and, thinking to give the visitor some walking room, she touched Brumus lightly with her toe and said sweetly, "Nice Brumus, come on and move now."

"Hey, look out—don't hurt him!" Bob said.

Angie was never sure how serious he was and she let it pass. The ambassador seemed just about to try a little jeté when Bob arose and Brumus did too and lumbered to his side.

Getting an ailing Brumus to the veterinarian was harder. Once, with Bob out of town, Ethel and the children undertook to do just that. The mistake was in using the convertible.

As soon as they drove down the driveway and turned into Chain Bridge Road, Brumus lurched and fell out of the car. A squeal of brakes, shouts, scrambling about and pushing and shoving got the world's biggest ragmop back aboard, and they were off again.

He fell out again. More shouting, scrambling, pushing and shoving, and this time, with everybody clutching Brumus, and Ethel driving very carefully, they made it to the vet.

12

Bobby's Zoo

President Kennedy's young administration confronted controversy at home and abroad. Freedom Riders protesting segregation were pulled from their buses and beaten in Alabama. Civil rights activists beseeched Robert Kennedy, as Attorney General, for protection, while segregationists blamed him, not the President, for "meddling" with their traditions. Abroad, the Soviets agreed with the United States to suspend all but underground nuclear tests. But the President's first effort at summitry, in Vienna, ended in heightened tensions. Soviet Premier Nikita S. Khrushchev rebuffed him, some said because he perceived him as too young and inexperienced, and talked threateningly. Relations with Cuba deteriorated dangerously.

Khrushchev precipitated the Berlin Crisis by proposing to sign a separate peace treaty with East Germany and oust the other World War II victors as occupying powers—America, Britain and France—from Germany. Kennedy rejected this and prepared to fight. He called up U.S. military reserves and launched nationwide construction of nuclear bomb shelters. Khrushchev canceled the nuclear test ban and built a wall to divide East and West Berlin. It was a Cold War stalemate. In Vietnam, Kennedy policies wavered between a State Department strategy to fight Communist guerrillas with economic aid and social change, and a Pen-

tagon push for more U.S. military involvement. Bob Kennedy, agonizing with his brother through all these crises, looked more than ever to Hickory Hill. There, he could shut out the world and share with his children the things they found important.

It all started with Berthie, the plush elephant. Young Bobby got her as a gift when he was four. They were inseparable until, as he grew older, live animals captured more and more of his attention.

In the beginning, though, even Ethel's gift of a second stuffed elephant named Bill, big enough for Bobby to ride, could not come between them. He took Berthie everywhere, even to bed in the room he shared with big brother Joe and he told her all the things he was thinking of.

"Bobby, I can't sleep," Joe would say. "You're making too much noise."

"I'm not talking to you," Bobby would say. "I'm talking to Berthie."

Edward R. Murrow, the Columbia Broadcasting System's celebrated commentator, visited Hickory Hill to do a "Person to Person" television show about the family. He lined up the children and had them all sitting together on the front steps. Bobby was clutching his stuffed pet.

"What's your elephant's name?" Murrow asked. When Bobby replied, "Berthie," Murrow asked him his own name.

"Robert Francis Kennedy, Junior," he replied. "I'm named after my daddy and Saint Francis. That's why I love animals. Saint Francis was very good with animals."

Kathleen spoke up. "You're making us miss our show," she told Murrow, and he asked, "Which one?"

"Mickey Mouse," she said.

Murrow, convulsed with laughter, excused the lot. They raced inside and put on their Mickey Mouse caps with the big ears and settled in a squirming mass around the TV set—even nanny Ena Bernard, who had a Mickey Mouse cap too—and

sang the song along with Annette Funicello and the gang:
"M - I - C - K - E - Y
"M - O - U - S - E !"

It was a natural role for Ena. She had taught all of them their ABCs in her own little preschool in the nursery. Her schedule for the little ones was rigid: As soon as they woke up, bathed and breakfasted, they were her pupils for about an hour. They worked at learning the alphabet and basic arithmetic before going outside to practice horseback riding or swimming or just to play.

Bobby's first live animals were two bantam chicks given him by a neighbor. He cobbled together a coop for them and, what with going to pet shops to keep them supplied, he developed an informed interest in animals in general. He especially liked reptiles and, while still in elementary school, got a job at the Washington National Zoo after class and on weekends, working with snakes, alligators, iguanas, lizards and the like. At first, he was a volunteer, but when the zoo people saw he was serious about animals, they put him on the payroll.

"He seems to like reptiles," a zookeeper told Ena. "He's very fond of these animals. And they don't hurt him."

Bob noticed too. He decided to surprise him with a mini zoo all his own, as a really big present for both Christmas and his birthday on January 17. Secretly, he set about having a terrarium built to accommodate a lot of small animals, with each kind enjoying its own special world. As it always seems to go with such things, the project kept growing until Bob found himself, despite expert guidance from people from a New York zoo, tearing out one whole side of the big new addition that Ethel had just completed to give Hickory Hill a proper living room.

"What's going on, Daddy?" Bobby, like all his brothers and sisters, wanted to know. "Why'd you break out the window?"

"Pipes," Bob said, not exactly an untruth. Another project in Ethel's remodeling of Hickory Hill was the addition of a sauna. "We've got to dig deep because of the pipes."

All told, about thirty-five various sorts of reptiles were moved in. A gift of an iguana from friends in Colombia added to the lot that summer. The box containing the iguana was delivered to the Kennedy compound at Hyannis Port and, when opened, proved to contain, not one, but eight iguanas.

"She had babies on the way up," Ena said. "First, we kept them in the big dollhouse to keep them warm, and then we put them in the attic. Lots of room in the attic for them to crawl around."

The children's governess then when the family summered at Hyannis Port, Eileen Hagen, loved animals as much as Bobby did. She undertook to care for all eight iguanas, even when one of them came down with what Ena called "the rotten jaw."

"While Bobby was away, she would take care of it. When he would come home, he'd look at me, but I'd say, 'No, Bobby, not me, I'm awfully sorry about your iguanas and the rotten jaw but I cannot bear to touch them.'"

Bobby seemed to acquire reptiles wherever he went. He returned from one trip to Puerto Rico with a snake in his coat pocket. It was small and nonpoisonous, but when he tried to show it off to his parents' dinner guests at Hickory Hill, most of them cleared out. One who did not flinch was Lydia Katzenbach, whose husband Nicholas was Bob Kennedy's deputy at the Justice Department.

"Oh, what a lovely snake," she said. She draped it around her neck and paraded around the room. "Look, everybody! Look at my lovely necklace!"

Bobby found few such sympathizers among grown-ups visiting Hickory Hill. K. LeMoyne Billings, an old family friend, had a particularly hard time with the snakes, for instance. The sight of one could set him to sweating and shaking. Billings was sixteen when he met John Kennedy at Choate, where they were roommates, and he met Bob on a visit to the Kennedy household. He was around so much thereafter that Patricia Kennedy Lawford once commented:

"Lem Billings was a close friend of both President Kennedy and Bobby—so close that he was almost raised with us. Mother thinks he was."

Billings was the godfather of young Bobby but no friend of his reptiles, even though he had arranged for the iguanas from Colombia. Later, perhaps trying to shift attention to more acceptable members of the animal world, he gave Bobby his first wild bird, a red-tailed hawk from Colombia.

But snakes remained Bobby's main preoccupation for a long time. A little black one that he found on the grounds of Hickory Hill was a particular bane for Billings. Bobby trained it to slither down from the treehouse of the big oak, up the back steps and into the house and then up the stairs to the second floor. After one confrontation on the stairway, Billings never left the guest room without careful reconnoitering beforehand. When the snake got into a fight with Bobby's Chinese dragon and lost, Billings shed no tears at the funeral.

"And there was a green one," Ena recalled. "Someone left the terrarium open and that green snake got out. It went into cook's room. The rug was green, a fuzzy rug, the same color as the snake. The cook was going on her day off and, while she was dressing, she noticed the rug moving just by her feet, and she bent over and looked and saw it was that green snake. She ran out of the room, screaming, 'I'm not working here any-more! There's a snake in my room!' And so we lost her."

His father also had some problems with the snakes, as Bobby recollected:

"Although I heard that some people called Daddy ruthless, I never saw any hint of this. He thought it cruel to feed live mice to snakes. He would never tolerate a live-animal eater as a pet."

As Bobby's interest shifted to include feathered creatures, Ethel contributed a pair of ring-necked pheasants in cages under the great oak. The hawk lived in Bobby's room and there was constant bickering over the mess it made there. Finally, reluctantly, he agreed to chain it up in the treehouse, which was really a full-scale model of the crimson triplane favored by Snoopy, the imaginative puppy in Charles M. Schulz's *Peanuts* comic strip, as the fanciful Red Baron of World War I.

"But the hawk was too close to where the pheasants were," Ena said. "One of them put his head out to get the grass, and the hawk flew down and got his head. When Bobby came home from school and found that out, he told the hawk, 'Now, I'm going to send you to school where you'll learn not to be so vicious.'"

Instead, he gave that hawk away to a friend and acquired some others, using the barn at Hickory Hill to keep them in and work with them. His favorite, a red-tailed hawk named Morgan Le Fay, was a special challenge. She had been taken from the nest and had never mastered the art of flight.

"Daddy was always deeply involved with everything his children were doing," Bobby recalled much later. "He was keenly interested in my experiences with my hawks and he frequently came down to the barn to see how I handled them. Daddy thought Morgan was useless because of her many unhawklike ways. Yet, he never tired of watching me work with her."

Bobby finally taught Morgan Le Fay how to fly. But, when she was about four years old, she flew off and never returned. Some children telephoned Hickory Hill to say they had seen her hovering about their school nearby. Bobby searched for days and finally concluded he would never again see his gentle friend:

"Either she went native or somebody shot her."

The turtle named Carruthers came from Kenya, which Bobby visited with his uncle, Sargent Shriver, then the first director of President Kennedy's Peace Corps. He brought the turtle back in a suitcase, making room for it by giving away his clothes. The payoff for him was that any turtle that could fill a suitcase should walk off with blue ribbons at family pet shows, the annual one at Hickory Hill as well as others in Hyannis Port, and Carruthers did, always honored as Biggest Turtle in Show.

He could have won the Congeniality Award too, according to Ena. He never snapped at anybody and all he did, really, was eat lettuce, carrots, cabbage and tomatoes, sleep a lot and walk around, mingling with Kennedys and their guests at Hickory Hill and Hyannis Port and sometimes Palm Beach and even patrolling the aisle of the family planes, the *Caroline* and *The Great Lakes.*

When Carruthers died, Bobby wanted Ena to take him to the Smithsonian Institution and have him preserved by a taxidermist. The Smithsonian, not overly intrigued, sent back word that this might require a little time, and Bobby, impatient, said:

"Okay. I know how to do it. Put him in a plastic bag and put him in the freezer."

Ena told Ethel that Carruthers had died, and she was very sad and solicitous for Bobby. She asked what he had done with him. When she heard, she said:

"What? In the freezer?"

When Bobby came home, he and his mother had a spirited conversation. Bobby later asked Ena:

"Please don't mention Carruthers and the freezer to Mommy anymore, because, you know, Mommy gets very nervous."

Carruthers, at last report, was still in a freezer somewhere.

David, a year and a half younger than Bobby, was strongly under his influence. He generally liked everything Bobby liked and tried to emulate him, just as his father had used his older brothers as role models. David soon got interested in unusual pets too, starting with a mountain goat, also a frequent flyer between Washington and Cape Cod, and a skunk, deodorized, a gift from his father and never one of Ena's favorites.

Courtney, almost three years younger than Bobby, brought home a pet of her own, a gift from one of the nuns at her school, Stone Ridge. It was a soft, fuzzy, warm, little white mouse that, unbeknownst to all, was in the family way. She had babies in Ethel's dressing room. One of them, tiny and pink, got away and started down the stairway just as Ethel began to walk up.

"Ena, something's on the stairs!" Ethel cried. "Get the exterminator!"

Courtney saved her brood. But she had to move them out of her mother's room and into the barn, where she continued to care for them until, one by one, they went off on their own.

Kerry, almost six years younger than Bobby, toddled after him on his wild animal hunts around Hickory Hill. Courtney had no interest in that, but Kerry was eager to go, up trees and under bushes looking for snakes, and in wet and muddy places in search of frogs and tadpoles. Bobby built a frog pond from a galvanized iron washtub, complete with an underground drain, about eight feet long, that he dug himself. He had little brother Michael, a year and a half older than Kerry, crawl through the tunnel to make sure it was in working order.

Once they caught a chipmunk, but it got away. So did the flying squirrel, a gift from a friend in North Carolina. They did better with the less skittish and more tamable sheep, goats and pigs.

Kerry took charge of the two pigs. They liked to run in the house, perhaps asserting rights in the old Irish tradition of pigs in the parlor, and she let them, until they grew too big. They began as little white pigs, but, as is their way, they grew into a problem. One simply disappeared one day and the other, the one named Flowers, was given away.

Dogs were always special at Hickory Hill, not only Brumus, the oafish Newfoundland, but particularly Freckles, the beguiling cocker spaniel, among the five or six always around. When Bob had something to think through, he would wander around Hickory Hill, tossing a football, accompanied by a canine entourage. The dogs seemed at such times to fall into his thoughtful mood. Young Bobby reminisced that his father "always had a very special way with animals" and "took great trouble with our dogs."

"The two of us competed over the love of our favorite dog, Freckles," he recalled. "Freckles spent most of his time with me. He slept in my room, went out for walks with me and, when I was in the car, Freckles was usually there. However, as soon as Daddy came home, Freckles never left his side. Even dogs that Daddy had never seen before would immediately like him. There was that certain something about him that even came through to animals."

Later on Bob took Freckles with him in 1968, stumping state caucuses and primaries in pursuit of the Democratic presidential nomination. John Glenn, the first American to orbit Earth and later a U.S. Senator and presidential aspirant himself, was along as a supporter. Glenn was a genuine asset. An international idol then, he had better name and face recognition than the candidate. He was always amazed at Freckles's aplomb amid the commotion of crowds, airplanes and motorcades.

"During one of the campaign swings through Nebraska, we rode through many crowds in the convertible with Bob sitting on one side of the back of the convertible and I on the other," Glenn remembered. "Freckles seemed to feel he was missing something and would hop up and sit between the two of us, just as though he was a third person, looking from side to side at the crowds along the street."

After a while, Bob leaned over to Glenn and whispered:

"The day I quit as a candidate is when Freckles starts shaking hands with the people."

Somewhere in Indiana, Freckles disappeared. Bob, carrying on with his five-speeches-a-day schedule, nevertheless was clearly distracted. He asked a half-dozen of us on the campaign to drop off and find Freckles. I looked around at my affluent colleagues—lawyers, bankers, entrepreneurs—and broke out laughing. It was a multimillion-dollar posse, perhaps the most moneyed, in terms of net worth, since Averell Harriman's father's hired guns went after Butch Cassidy and the Sundance Kid for robbing the Union Pacific.

Once, after he had thanked me for a favor, I said jokingly

that, if he were truly grateful, he could prove it after he was President by appointing me Ambassador to Ireland. As our search party fanned out to look for his dog, he tapped my arm and said:

"Find Freckles, or you'll be lucky to get Luxembourg."

We found Freckles, left behind at the last stop.

I asked Bob if he promised Ireland to everybody on the tour of Irish ancestry, and he grinned wordlessly.

13

Ena Bernard

Soviet Premier Nikita S. Khrushchev followed the Berlin Crisis by testing President Kennedy closer to home. He secretly installed nuclear missiles in Cuba. He withdrew them only after Kennedy threatened nuclear retaliation against Moscow if any Cuba-based nuclear missiles hit the United States. Conciliatorily, U.S. missiles were withdrawn from Turkey. Attorney General Robert Kennedy was his brother's chief strategist in the Cuban Missile Crisis as the world teetered on the brink of nuclear war. In the aftermath, the Kennedys arranged Cuba's first release of prisoners taken in the disastrous Bay of Pigs landing. The Kennedy civil rights legislation stalled in Congress. At Hickory Hill, the children complained to Ethel Kennedy that their father was away from home too much.

Bob Kennedy called Ena Bernard "our treasure." She joined the family as a nursemaid in 1952 and she stayed on at Hickory Hill as a member of the family long after the eleventh and last of her charges, Rory, had grown to maturity. Bob always said that whatever Ena wanted Ena would get because the family could not function without her.

Ena was indeed Ethel's secret weapon. As Bob's sister, Patricia Kennedy Lawford, observed:

"Everyone who wondered how Ethel could raise eleven children knew when they saw Ena in action."

Ena took her cues from Bob mostly, but she learned early on that, in the division of labor at Hickory Hill, Ethel was always in charge of bathing the babies. One morning, though, Ethel went to the nursery and there was no baby to bathe. Bob had, on impulse, taken tiny Max to his office.

"But, Mr. Kennedy," Ena had protested, "he hasn't had his bath yet. You can't take a baby out when he needs a bath."

"He's fine," Bob said. "I won't tell anybody he's unclean and nobody will notice. We'll throw a little talcum on him."

Ethel had a touch of panic when she discovered Max missing. She felt a sudden clutch at her heart. There had been threats from time to time and the fear of kidnapping was never far from her thoughts. She was annoyed at Bob when Ena told her what he had done. But she forgave him in the next breath, as always, and, when Bob sent Max home in late morning, she gave him his bath then.

Bob worked late that night and, as usual, he telephoned just before leaving the office, near midnight, to say:

"Please don't call Mrs. Kennedy. Please don't let her know I'm on my way."

That put Ena in a bind. Ethel had given her strict orders to wake her at any time, day or night, when Bob was coming from the office or returning from an out-of-town trip. She impressed on Ena that her desire to greet Bob was stronger than her need for rest, no matter what he might say.

Ena got no such mixed signals on the rights of the children. She saw clearly that nothing gave Bob more pleasure or had a higher priority for him than his children.

"When he was Attorney General and he worked very late, he'd invite the children to his office to have lunch or dinner—really great fun for them, they loved it," she remembered, and that led her to recall what he had told her about the protocol to follow when parties were held at Hickory Hill:

"Ena, I want the children to come down and say good night. I don't care who it is we have as guests. Always have the children come down, even the little baby."

Ena took over where Luella Hennessey left off. Luella was the registered nurse the Kennedys called in whenever anybody was about to be born. Starting with Bob and Ethel's first, Kathleen, she was in attendance at twenty-seven Kennedy births, all told.

Bob more or less adopted Luella Hennessey when he was twelve years old and hospitalized with pneumonia at St. Elizabeth's Hospital in Brighton, Massachusetts. Pat Kennedy was there too, recovering from an appendectomy, and Luella was taking care of her. When it came time to go home to Hyannis Port, they persuaded their parents to keep Luella on. Soon they parlayed that into having her accompany the family to London, where their father was U.S. Ambassador to Great Britain.

"Whenever Luella's blue Ford appeared outside a maternity hospital," Pat once said, "you could be sure another Kennedy was on the way."

Luella was certain for a long time that Bob would become a priest because of "his great love for people," apparent even then. Disappointed, she reconciled herself that Bob was in the "lay apostolate." And she could back up that assessment with a seemingly endless supply of stories. One of them:

"When Bobby and Ethel's first child, Kathleen, was born in Greenwich, Connecticut, Bobby asked me to fly [from Boston] to New York, meet him there, and then proceed to the hospital to care for Ethel. But in those days, I didn't like to fly alone. What did he do? He flew into Logan Airport, and after a ten-minute interval, we both boarded the next flight to New York."

Ena had to laugh at Bob's approach to the babies. He treated them like eggshells that might crack in his hands if he were not careful. He never failed to visit the baby's room when he came home from work, but he was always tentative and restrained, a far cry from the roughhouse approach he took with the older children. With them, it was all jostling and giggling, pulling and pushing, tickling and teasing, as if he were one of them and not the father.

"I think Mr. Kennedy was kind of scared he'd drop the babies," Ena said. "He would stand back a little ways and say, 'How is my little girl?' or 'How is my little fella?' and talk to them that way for à little while. When he picked them up, he held them very gingerly."

Anybody who saw Bob Kennedy with his children, or anybody else's children, for that matter, would have to agree with Ena. He looked awkward holding a baby, usually handing off quickly to Ethel or Ena or whoever else was nearby, but he was completely at ease with the older ones, as a friend, an equal and not a father. They adored him for it, battling to reach him first when he returned from a trip.

It was indeed an experience to whip into the horseshoe driveway at Hickory Hill with him at such a time. Before he could get out of the car, the front door of the house would burst open and the Kennedy horde would fly out in a howling, pell-mell stampede. Journalist Peter Hamill observed that Bob looked then like a man being overrun by a giant centipede.

In Ena's considerable memory, there never was a time that Bob came home saying he was too tired or too busy for the children. Shaving in the morning, even, he would have children all over him, smearing shaving cream on him and on themselves.

"After the children started growing and walking, then he would start doing things with them," she said. "He would take them swimming or play football or read them stories or tell them stories about his life, or about people in different countries.

"One thing I noticed was his interest in the people of Africa. He used to tell the children a lot about Africa. Once they had a movie called *Africa Speaks*. He had all the children watch the movie and from that time I noticed that little Bobby got very much interested in Africa and he still is today."

Bob Kennedy used the dinner table as a children's seminar, just as his father had done, and sometimes as a kind of family council. He would provoke discussions on government, history, religion—what Ena called "all the important things"—and when there had been a major event, he would say:

"What happened today? Did you read the newspapers?"

Each child would try to give an answer, and he would quiz them and help them along. Or he would ask their advice on something he was planning to do.

"I remember one day at the table in particular," Ena laughed. "Mr. Kennedy said, 'Well, children, how would you like it if Daddy runs for senator from New York?'

"They all said, 'Oh, Daddy, we don't want to live in New York! Could we stay here and at the Cape?'

"He told them yes, they could, and with that they gave him their endorsement."

President Harry Truman once said he never had any problems managing children and he could not understand why anybody else did. "I just find out what they want," he said, "and I give it to them." Bob Kennedy's way with children might have been something like that, but, because there was a part of him that never ceased being a child, he sometimes knew better than the children what they wanted. Yet, he avoided forcing anything on them, and with his gentle prodding they seemed to get to where they were going on their own.

David loved football, and so Bob took him to the Washington Redskins games whenever he could. He took Joe too, when he was home, because he also liked football, and in prep school played it until he broke a leg. That was in Joe's awkward early adolescence, a time when Bob once sighed:

"Poor kid, at that age, he can't seem to walk across the room without knocking over a coffee table. I was pretty much the same way."

For Kathleen, it was horses, and Bob and Ethel consequently logged a lot of time at horse shows. Little Bobby was a holy terror in family touch football, but his real interest lay with small animals, the more exotic the better.

"Mr. Kennedy taught the children courage by doing things with them, like swimming or football or even climbing on the roof," Ena said. "He gave them faith in themselves and they weren't afraid."

Two special kindnesses stand out above many in Ena's recollection. Her stories illustrate two facets of Bob's character, perhaps actually both sides of the same coin: the genuine respect he accorded children of all ages and the coercive effect he could have on children without raising his hand or his voice.

"He was thoughtful about including me in everything the family did—he even arranged for me to go home to Costa Rica when President Kennedy made a trip there for the Alliance for Progress," she said, smiling, warmed by the memory. "It was in all the newspapers in Costa Rica and it made the people love President Kennedy and the whole Kennedy family that a Costa Rican should be honored like that."

The other time came when she brought her daughter Josefina from Costa Rica. Bob accepted Fina as one of his own, Ena said, and drove them some three hundred miles to put her in a good school—one hundred and fifty miles to St. Francis de Sales in Roanoke, Virginia, and back again in one day. The next year, it was Bob's idea to register her closer to home. Overriding segregationist barriers still around in Washington at that time, he enrolled her in Gordon Junior High School and, later, in Western High School.

"She was the first black student at both schools," Ena said, "even though at Gordon they wouldn't put her picture in the yearbook."

Later, Fina stayed with her mother at Hickory Hill.

"One night she came home very late, later than she had promised," Ena recalled. "Mr. Kennedy asked her to come and speak to him when she came in.

"He said, 'Fina, do you have anything to say?'

Early on, Bobby was protective of little brother Teddy. *Courtesy JFK Library, JPK Enterprises*

The 1947 Harvard football team. End Robert Kennedy is far right in the front row, quarterback Kenneth O'Donnell second from left in the back row. *Courtesy JFK Library*

Ethel and Bobby, surrounded by other Kennedys, including a future President, take the cake at their June wedding in 1950. *Courtesy JFK Library*

A visit from Grandpa. Kathleen, Bobby Jr., and Joseph III, with their proud parents at their home in Washington's Georgetown.
Courtesy JFK Library

The brothers Kennedy at Hickory Hill. The smooth one is President, the leafy one Attorney General. *Courtesy JFK Library*

Chief Counsel Robert Kennedy of the Senate Rackets Committee confronts Teamsters President James R. Hoffa with committee investigator Walter Sheridan. *Courtesy JFK Library, © UPI*

Bedtime prayers. Courtney, David, Bobby Jr., Joseph III, and Kathleen follow Bob and Ethel. Some blessings called down on the family ended "...and whatever God sends." Translation: Another child on the way.

Courtesy JFK Library, © Jacques Lowe

Ena Bernard came to Hickory Hill as an employee, stayed as a friend long after helping Ethel raise eleven Kennedys. Here, she and Christopher share a tender moment. Bob called Ena "our treasure."

Courtesy Ethel Kennedy

Whatever he did, slamming a tennis ball or running for President, Bobby put all of himself into it. *Art Rickerby, LIFE magazine © Time Warner Inc.*

All-Kennedy Touch. Bob passes to David against defenders Bobby Jr., behind him, as Michael grimaces. Brumus the feisty Newfoundland referees. *Courtesy JFK Library, © Elizabeth Kuhner*

Bob had never shot the rapids in a kayak before, reason enough to try.
Courtesy JFK Library

He was afraid of horses,
but only for a while.
Courtesy JFK Library

The first to climb Mt. Kennedy. He prepared, he told Everest conqueror Jim Whittaker, by running up Hickory Hill's stairs and yelling, "Help!"
Courtesy JFK Library

Eight little Kennedys act out a special nativity scene, with various pets, Brumus front and center. *Courtesy JFK Library, © Elizabeth Kuhner*

Bob Kennedy in his element, clowning amid children and dogs at Hickory Hill.
Courtesy JFK Library, © Elizabeth Kuhner

Columnists Art
Buchwald, Rowland
Evans, and Phil
Geyelin, properly
dressed as Hickory
Hill Pet Show
judges, ponder who
should win the
Smallest Fish
Award.
© Melody Miller

Ethel, Bob, and their brood pose at the pond on Hickory Hill's newly installed terrace. *Courtesy JFK Library*

A family affair. Bob is joined in 1968 run for the presidency by Ethel and some of their children. Bill Barry steadies Bob, as he did throughout. *Bill Eppridge,* LIFE *magazine* © *Time Warner Inc.*

Freckles the spaniel enjoys a respite from rigorous campaigning in 1968. *Courtesy JFK Library, © Burt Berinsky*

David Hackett, Bob's best friend from prep school days, watches California election returns in the Ambassador Hotel campaign suite with Jean Kennedy Smith and other Kennedys, on the fateful night of June 4, 1968. *Bill Eppridge, LIFE magazine © Time Warner Inc.*

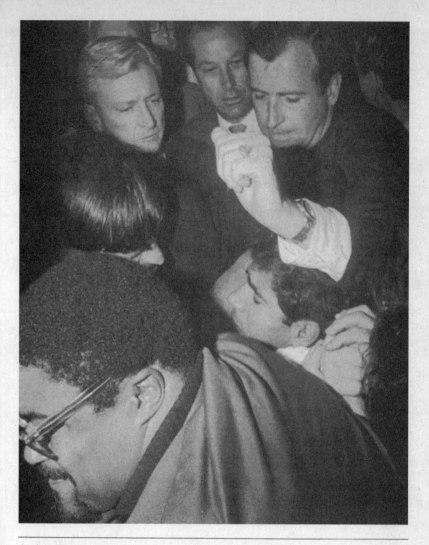

Author Warren Rogers wrestled with Sirhan Sirhan, Bob Kennedy's assassin, in the Ambassador Hotel seconds after the shots. Others in the melee include Roosevelt Grier, George Plimpton, Dun Gifford, and Paul Hope. © *UPI*

After funeral services at St. Patrick's Cathedral in New York, Bill Barry leads the way for Ethel, Joe III, Ted, Mrs. Rose Kennedy, and Bobby Jr. *Herbert Scharfman, LIFE magazine © Time Warner Inc..*

The people say good-bye. Thousands turned out to line the tracks from New York City to Washington, D.C., as the funeral train bore Bob Kennedy to rest in Arlington National Cemetery. *Courtesy JFK Library*

Wherever he went, Bob Kennedy was drawn to the poor, the lonely, the downtrodden, and he met them on their own terms, eye to eye. *Courtesy JFK Library,* © *George Ballis*

"She just stood and looked at him and he said, 'Well, what time were you supposed to come in?'

"She said, 'I was supposed to be in by eleven. I'm sorry.'

"And he said, 'Never let that happen again because you worried your mother.'

"Afterward, Fina said, 'I'll never forget what Mr. Kennedy did for me as long as I live.'

"He showed that interest. He treated her as a father would."

It was not always easy being one of Bob Kennedy's children. Early on they saw he set impossibly high standards, refused to be daunted by them and insisted that no Kennedy, whether his own or another Kennedy's or one brought into the fold like Fina, could do less.

"A Kennedy doesn't cry," he would say. And, "A Kennedy never gives up."

It was one thing for him to live by those spartan rules, but it was quite another for little boys and girls who, in other circumstances, would have been content to be quite ordinary, failing and learning to live with failure. Once, as he sought the Democratic presidential nomination in 1968, he sat down next to me on the campaign plane and said:

"Let me tell you a funny story. I was trying to teach my little nephew John how to kick a football. He's pretty little and he couldn't get the hang of it. He'd kick and the ball wouldn't go far and he'd fall down. Or it would go over his head backwards and he'd fall down. Or he'd miss it altogether and fall down. Each time I'd say, 'Get up, try again,' and he would.

"That went on for a while, and then he stayed down. I said, 'Get up, try again.' He didn't budge. I said, 'Come on, a Kennedy never gives up.' And he said, 'Hmmph, here's one that does.' Isn't that funny? Kids are great."

And there was the time he was struggling with indecision over whether to run for President and I was dogging him on a cover story for *LOOK* magazine. We got out of his car at his

Senate office building. On the sidewalk outside were two little street urchins about nine or ten. Shyly, the boys sidled up to him, and Bob, squatting to be at eye level, warmly greeted the one he knew. That one said to the other:

"Joey, I want you to meet Senator Kennedy, my friend."

14

Jack

*President Kennedy's third year in office found him looking back at a begin-
ning crammed with crises, over Communist pressures abroad and civil rights
strife at home, and with his administration's record in coping mixed at best.
In his third year, as he started planning a 1964 reelection campaign, things
began to look a little better. The United States, Britain and the Soviet
Union agreed to ban all but underground nuclear testing. The Supreme
Court ruled all criminal defendants must have counsel and rejected illegally
acquired evidence as inadmissible in either state or federal court. The civil
rights leader, Dr. Martin Luther King, Jr., made his "I have a dream"
speech at Washington's Lincoln Memorial to two hundred thousand demon-
strators demanding equal rights for minorities. The President curtailed support for South Vietnam's President Ngo Dinh Diem, and a military coup
erupted, the leaders taking power and killing Diem. By then, American
troops in Vietnam numbered fifteen thousand and U.S. economic and military aid totaled five hundred million dollars. Kennedy, his eye on 1964,
booked a quick trip to Texas to try to end friction between Democratic fac-
tions there. Highlight of the trip was to be a speech in Dallas. Bob
Kennedy considered the approach of middle age as he celebrated his thirty-
eighth birthday, determined to move his life in a new direction.*

*   *   *

Bob was troubled as his brother's presidency neared the end of its third year. He had managed the campaign that put Jack in the White House. He had then served him well, as Attorney General and as his most valuable adviser and most trusted confidant. They had steered a sometimes uneven, sometimes brilliant, but always courageous course through such crises as the Bay of Pigs, the Cuba missile confrontation and civil rights strife in the South, plus initiatives like the Alliance for Progress in Latin America, the Peace Corps worldwide and a program to put a man on the moon. Much more waited to be done.

Now, as he contemplated the ordeal of a reelection campaign scant months away, Bob began to turn inward, shutting out others, brooding about his future and his brother's. In such a mood, Ethel commented, he was "no barrel of laughs." At dinner or sitting around, he would suddenly go silent, lost in thought, insensitive to everything around him. She knew the mood and she did the best she could to force her sunny nature to cope with it.

Bob did not intend to run the 1964 campaign or to stay in the administration after Jack's expected reelection. He had talked to Ethel about moving on to other vistas, as yet undefined, perhaps in publishing or education. The Third World attracted him. His visits to Latin America as part of President Kennedy's Alliance for Progress undertaking had especially piqued his interest. Ethel was, as in all things, ready to follow wherever he led.

Bob said his blunt ways and high visibility, notably in stirring Southern enmity over equal rights, had created political obstacles for Jack that only his departure could remove. Polls indicated he probably was right.

Sister Jean's husband, Stephen Smith, began fund raising and organizing, preparing to step in as 1964 campaign manager. At one meeting, Jack teased Bob about his unpopularity, especially among white Southerners, and suggested they could make their point and enliven the campaign if he and Bob got into a public fight. On the serious side, Bob considered resigning before the campaign began.

Bob celebrated his thirty-eighth birthday three times on November 20, 1963. At a Justice Department party, he climbed on his desk, a practice when his office filled with schoolchildren or other visitors, to give a wry little speech about what a political asset he was. At the White House, he attended a reception for the judiciary, going upstairs afterward to talk with the President and his wife. He found both excited about their upcoming trip to Texas. Ethel arrived to drag him off to Hickory Hill and the big party she had for him there.

They finally got to bed at three, when she remembered to tell him of her birthday surprise, a sauna in the basement.

Two days later, he was having a poolside lunch at Hickory Hill with Ethel, U.S. Attorney Robert Morgenthau of New York and Silvio Mollo, head of Morgenthau's criminal division. He had brought the two men over from a Washington meeting for a swim and clam chowder and tuna fish sandwiches. It was sunny and unseasonably warm for November, but only Bob had actually gone swimming.

Down the sloping lawn from the house came the faint sounds of a transistor radio. Painters were putting a second coat on the big new wing that was Ethel's pride. A little after one-thirty, Bob said they had better be getting back.

Just then, Morgenthau saw one of the painters come running toward the pool, waving a little hand-held radio and shouting incomprehensibly. At the same time, a maid ran down, saying, "Mr. Hoover's on the White House phone." An extension telephone rang across the pool and Ethel went over and picked it up.

"It's J. Edgar Hoover," she called to Bob.

Morgenthau suddenly understood what the painter was shouting:

"They say the President's been shot."

On the phone, Bob recalled later, Hoover said:

"I have news for you. The President's been shot. I think it's serious. I'll call you back . . . when I find out more."

Morgenthau watched Bob put down the phone, turn away and clap his hand to his mouth. Ethel saw the look on her husband's face and went to his side. For a few seconds, they stood like that. And then Bob said:

"Jack's been shot. It may be fatal."

They walked to the house. Morgenthau and Mollo went to a television set in the living room and Bob and Ethel went upstairs. There, Bob called Dallas trying to reach Kenneth O'Donnell, who headed the White House staff. He had no luck, but Clint Hill of the Secret Service told him the President's wounds looked fatal.

Numb, Bob and Ethel changed the subject to Hoover, who never hid his resentment of Bob's efforts to curb his power. How cold Hoover had been, Bob said, and how he seemed to savor telling him that Jack was shot. Ethel nodded. She had made only one visit to Hoover's office, a courtesy call when Bob became Attorney General and nominally Hoover's boss. Hoover had been cold then, she recalled, and never acknowledged all the little Kennedys crawling over his furniture and falling into his giant flowerpots. Leaving, Ethel had scribbled a note and slipped it into an FBI suggestion box: "Chief Parker of Los Angeles for FBI Director."

Morgenthau said later he wanted to leave but felt Bob and Ethel should not be left alone. Upstairs, Bob talked on the telephone some more to Dallas. He came down and told Morgenthau:

"He's dead."

People began arriving: Director John McCone, from the Central Intelligence Agency less than a mile away, Supreme Court Justice Byron White, old football friends David Hackett and Dean Markham, and Edwin O. Guthman, Bob's press secretary and confidant.

"How are you doing?" Bob greeted Guthman.

"I've seen better days," Ed replied.

"Don't be gloomy," Bob said. "That's one thing I don't need now."

They went out to the lawn behind the house, Guthman following along as Bob strode back and forth, back and forth. Already, it seemed, he was beginning to blame himself for not preventing his brother's death. He had grown used to protecting Jack in all things, smoothing his way, taking his blows.

"There's so much bitterness," Bob said. "I thought they would get one of us. But Jack, after all he'd been through, never worried about it."

They walked on, wordlessly. When he spoke again, his voice was strained and expressionless:

"I'd received a letter from someone in Texas last week warning me not to let the President go to Dallas because they would kill him. I sent it to Kenny O'Donnell, but I never thought it would happen. I thought it would be me. There's been so much bitterness and hatred, and so many people who might have said something have remained silent. . . . "

Guthman searched agonizingly for a word of comfort. He said hopefully that perhaps the country would unite now, that maybe people would learn from the enormity of the tragedy and there would be less bitterness in the land.

"No," Bob said. "This will make it worse."

In some quarters, at least, he was proved right immediately.

James Hoffa put out a statement saying the assassination made Bob Kennedy "just another lawyer." And, with almost every flag in the country lowered to half-staff, Hoffa ordered the one at Teamsters headquarters on Capitol Hill run up to the top of the pole and kept there.

15

Bob Alone

After the assassination of President Kennedy, Vice President Lyndon B. Johnson also expedited hearings by a commission, headed by U.S. Supreme Court Chief Justice Earl Warren, that investigated the Kennedy assassination and found that Lee Harvey Oswald was solely responsible for it. Johnson faced crises in Panama, where anti-U.S. riots led to a Washington offer to negotiate a new Panama Canal treaty, and in Southeast Asia, where American involvement deepened. Johnson sent military planes to Laos and, after two U.S. destroyers reported being attacked by two North Vietnamese boats, Congress passed the Tonkin Resolution authorizing presidential action in Vietnam. Bob Kennedy was still Attorney General but no longer the No. 1 presidential adviser. He was, in fact, as brushed aside in the Johnson administration as Vice President Johnson felt he had been in the Kennedy administration.

After President Kennedy's funeral, Bob and Ethel went to the family's Palm Beach, Florida, home for a few days. When they returned, Guthman and others close to him were shocked at Bob's appearance and manner. He was ashen and melancholy, dark glasses shading swollen, haunted eyes, and he would sit staring into space for long moments, hands on his lap, palms up and lifeless. He rejected solace, holding his grief behind a wall of silence. Only Ethel, his brother and sisters and Jacqueline could reach him.

On December 5, Jacqueline Kennedy moved out of the White House to a Georgetown house that Averell Harriman provided. The same day, Bob wrote to Guthman and others who had served the New Frontier. On White House stationery in his small, cramped handwriting, he said:

> This is the last day in the White House and I
> did not want it to pass without thanking you on
> behalf of the President and myself for all that
> you have done over the past three years.
>
> Best,
>
> Bob

Guthman, a good and gentle but determined man, did what he could. At the Justice Department, he kept bringing papers to Bob for study and signature. But they would accumulate on his desk. Guthman brought in other aides who had worked closely with Bob over the years. He called reporters who knew Bob well and asked them to come in and ask Bob questions. Some of us did.

I protested to Guthman that I really had no business with the Attorney General at that time, nothing going on at the Justice Department that I wanted to write about. Besides, I said, I did not want to intrude.

"You won't be intruding," Ed said. "Just come over. Ask him anything. Just get him interested in something and talking. Draw him out of the damned shell he's in."

Bob received me pleasantly, but it was obvious he was simply going through the motions, not really hearing what I was saying to him, grunting generalities in response out of politeness. I think he knew what Guthman was up to, but he went along because it did not really matter to him what he did with his time. It was hard to sit with him like that, in that office that had known so much joy and energy, and to fail so miserably to arouse him.

Murray Kempton of the *New York Post* also obliged. He was shocked to see Bob looking as if his shirt collar and suit jacket were a couple of sizes too large. Kempton said he seemed to be withdrawing rather than shrinking. Peter Maas, another New York reporter, flew to Washington and accompanied him to a Christmas party for orphans organized by Mary McGrory, then of the *Washington Star*. Maas reported:

"The moment we walked in the room, all these little children—screaming and playing—there was just suddenly silence. Everybody was still . . . all standing there, and the adults too, and I was standing off to one side. Bob stepped into the middle of the room and just then, a little boy—I don't suppose he was more than six or seven years old—suddenly darted forward, and stopped in front of him, and said, 'Your brother's dead! Your brother's dead!'

"Gosh, you know, you could hear a pin drop. The adults, all of us, we just kind of turned away . . . you know, to the wall. The little boy knew he had done something wrong, but he didn't know *what*. So he started to cry. Bobby stepped forward and picked him up, in kind of one motion, and held him very close for a moment, and he said, 'That's all right. I have another brother.'"

Bob finally began pulling himself together—and in a characteristic way. He asked employees at the Justice Department to join with him in giving a memorable Christmas party for poor children. John T. Duffner, an assistant to Deputy Attorney General Nicholas DeB. Katzenbach, volunteered to organize and coordinate the affair and, taking his cue from Bob, he went all-out.

Duffner welcomed the chance to do anything that might

help snap the Attorney General out of his depression. Like other careerists, he had been skeptical of a boss so young, so inexperienced and so wired in at the White House, but Bob's out-of-the-ordinary approach won him over. His first surprise had come when Bob sent complimentary messages on February 23, 1961, barely a month after taking over. He thanked all those he assumed had worked the previous day even though it was George Washington's birthday, a government holiday, because their cars were recorded parked in the Justice Department garage.

What Bob did not know was that most of them had dropped their cars off, while they shopped for bargains at the city's traditional Washington's Birthday sales, and did not go near their offices. Nevertheless, the psychology worked. A feeling spread that good work would be appreciated, and it became common for people to work on their days off without making a fuss about it.

Bob gave Duffner five specifications for the Christmas party: He wanted it held on the afternoon of Friday, December 20; he wanted the children to come from schools in the poorest areas; he wanted them riding in sleighs on snow, real if possible and artificial if necessary, and he wanted to shake hands with each and every child.

Duffner pitched in, almost overwhelmed with volunteer help, and, as he recalled later—this happened at the Justice Department:

"Seven hundred children came. They rode in sleighs on a courtyard covered with manufactured snow, or a mule-drawn, red coach. They received presents, ate ice cream, popcorn and candy, and watched a show emceed by James Symington (then a Justice Department aide and later a U.S. Congress member from Missouri) and featuring Carol Channing and the Smothers Brothers in the Great Hall.

"There were musicians, magicians, clowns and [Washington Redskins] football players—Bobby Mitchell, Norm Snead, Vince Promuto, Andy Stynchula and Andy Davis. Animal-clad figures roamed the building. Augmented by two Keystone Cops, they helped direct the children through the corridors from the Great Hall to the Attorney General's office and back again."

The football players, wearing Santa Claus hats, drove the three horse-drawn sleighs. A Washington ice company had blown five inches of artificial snow onto the courtyard. So many employees showed up to help that U.S. marshals had to clear the way for the children. In the Great Hall, they all sat on the floor and joined in Christmas carols. Carol Channing sang "Hello, Dolly" and "Diamonds Are a Girl's Best Friend" and nearly caused a riot when she offered eighteen Dolly dolls, one for each school represented, and tossed out "diamond" bracelets made real, she said, by all the love behind them.

Ethel was there with a collection of Kennedy children. They all stood with Bob near a fabricated chimney top loaded with toys that were handed out by a Snow Queen and a tiger. Four-year-old Kerry Kennedy accused the tiger of being a man in disguise and, when he raised his paw tigerlike, she lectured, "You're not supposed to do that." Bob spoke briefly, about the need for love all year round and not only at Christmas, and introduced the star of the show, Santa Claus, played by his aide Barney Ross, who had served aboard John Kennedy's PT-109 and was marooned with him when a Japanese destroyer rammed and sank it in World War II.

Hundreds of thank-you letters poured in from the fourth, fifth and sixth graders who attended the party, and Bob kept them all.

Bob made his first public speech since President Kennedy's assassination on Saint Patrick's Day, March 17, 1964, in Scranton, Pennsylvania, to the Friendly Sons of Saint Patrick of Lackawanna County. When press secretary Guthman brought him a draft, Bob added the entire ballad about Owen Roe O'Neill, the seventeenth century champion of Irish independence, that laments, "Oh, why did you leave us, Owen? Why did you die?" When he reworked the draft, Guthman omitted the poem.

"Why did you do that?" Bob asked.

"You'll never get through it," Guthman said. "You don't have to put yourself through that."

"I've been practicing," Bob said. "I've been practicing in front of a mirror. I can't get through it yet, but I will."

In Scranton he did, and everyone in the place knew he was talking about his fallen brother:

> Sagest in the council was he,
> Kindest in the Hall;
> Sure we never won a battle
> Owen won them all.
> Soft as woman's was your voice, O'Neill.
> Bright was your eye.
> O! Why did you leave us, Owen?
> Why did you die?

> Your troubles are all over.
> You're at rest with God on high.
> But we're slaves, and we're orphans, Owen!
> Why did you die?
> We're sheep without a shepherd,
> When the snow shuts out the sky.
> Oh! Why did you leave us, Owen?
> Why did you die?

"Bob could do anything he set his mind on," Guthman said.

Bob came to reading late, which is to say that, like most American boys of his generation, he read what he had to read to get by in school. There was little reading for pleasure and even then he usually chose light fare. But, after law school and while conducting Senate investigations, he moved up in quality, first devouring job-related materials and then foraging to satisfy a growing hunger for knowledge for its own sake. After President Kennedy's death, his reading tended toward the philosophical, the healing word and the self-improving, and he began also to pursue poetry, memorizing long passages and pondering them. He was never without a book then, on his desk, in his briefcase, in his coat pocket, always the written word near at hand.

One quotation from Theodore Roosevelt he liked so much that, in time, he had it engraved on a plaque and put up alongside the door of his Senate office:

It is not the critic who counts. The credit belongs to the man who is actually in the arena—whose face is marred by dust and sweat and blood, who at the best knows in the end the triumph of high achievement and who at the worst if he fails at least fails while daring greatly so that his place will never be with those cold and timid souls who know neither victory nor defeat.

Jacqueline Kennedy gave him a copy of Edith Hamilton's *The Greek Way* and he read it over and over, underlining passages about suffering and fighting against odds. He read Thucydides and he memorized famous lines from Aeschylus and Sophocles. He also took up Shakespeare and George Bernard Shaw and he began memorizing extensively from Albert Camus. A favorite, which he later used in speeches:

Perhaps we cannot prevent this world from being a world in which children are tortured. But we can reduce the number of tortured children. And if you believers don't help us, who else in the world can help us do this?

He read Ralph Waldo Emerson over and over. On his desk at Hickory Hill was a book of Emerson essays with three passages marked in the margin: "This time, like all times, is a very good one, if we but know what to do with it," said one passage. Another said, "If the single man plant himself on his instincts, and there abide, the huge world will come round to him." And the other:

The characteristic of heroism is its persistency. All men have wandering impulses, fits and starts of generosity. But when you have chosen your part, abide by it, and do not weakly try to reconcile yourself with the world. The heroic cannot be the common, nor the common the heroic. Yet we have the weakness to expect the sympathy of people in those actions whose excellence is that they outrun sympathy and appeal to a tardy justice.

If you would serve your brother, because it is fit for you to serve him, do not take back your words when you find that prudent people do not commmend you. Adhere to your own act, and congratulate yourself if you have done something strange and extravagant and broken the monotony of a decorous age.

It was a high counsel that I once heard given to a young person, "Always do what you are afraid to do."

16

The Horse Thief

President Johnson rejected Robert Kennedy's request to accept him as his vice presidential running mate in the 1964 presidential election, choosing Hubert Humphrey instead. Bob ran for the U.S. Senate from New York and won. The Vietnam War overwhelmingly occupied Johnson's attention. He began the continuous bombing of the North, first below the 20th parallel and then of Hanoi itself. U.S. force levels in Vietnam rose to 184,300 in 1965 and then to 385,300 by the end of 1966, with another 100,000 offshore and in Thailand. U.S. forces began firing into Cambodia. At home, blacks in Los Angeles's Watts area rioted, causing thirty-five deaths and two hundred million dollars in property damage. Johnson sent 14,000 troops to the Dominican Republic during civil war there. The President pressed his Great Society programs for health and welfare. Congress approved President Truman's old dream of Medicare, through which the government paid part of the medical expenses of people over sixty-five. Johnson's tense relations with Bob Kennedy worsened with publication of a book about President Kennedy, written by William Manchester with family cooperation, that depicted Johnson unflatteringly. In the 1966 congressional elections, Bob Kennedy toured the country speaking on behalf of Democratic candidates, but also testing the wind for a run against Johnson for the presidency in 1968.

The penalty for stealing a horse in Virginia at that time was death by hanging. Ethel Kennedy did not know this when she took Nicholas N. Zemo's neglected horse from a dilapidated chicken coop on his farm and set it up in her stable at Hickory Hill with feed, water, blankets and an attending veterinarian. But that was the law, and ignorance of the law is no excuse. She did not take the matter lightly.

Breeder Zemo had an old score to settle with Ethel when he accused her of, in effect, stealing his horse. She had blown the whistle on him in 1963 and, after two years of smarting, he filed suit against her for thirty thousand dollars in damages. The case came to trial more than a year later, by which time Ethel, at thirty-eight, was seven months pregnant with Douglas, her tenth child.

She had the sympathy vote hands down when she swept into the Fairfax County Courthouse to testify on January 9, 1967. Fresh from Christmas skiing at Averell Harriman's Sun Valley resort in Idaho, she was "tanned and chipper," according to court reporters, in "a plain blue maternity dress with a double strand of pearls and a jeweled pin." She did not look like a horse thief.

Bob Kennedy escorted his wife to the courtroom, turned her over to her attorneys, Louis Oberdorfer, Jr., one of his top assistants at the Justice Department and later a federal judge, and Carrington Williams. He quickly retreated to his Senate office. There, earlier, as he took the case, Oberdorfer had echoed the friendly sentiments that Ethel had aroused at the courthouse:

"Who could believe Ethel Kennedy could steal a horse?"

"I could," Bob had mumbled.

Ethel's brush with the law began October 8, 1963, when she set out with several of her children on horseback through the woodlands around Hickory Hill. Trotting near Central Intelligence Agency headquarters in Langley, they cut across some property on Virginia State Route 193.

They heard a noise and pulled up. It sounded like a horse in trouble, and it was coming from a low, dirty shed that looked as if it might once have housed chickens. Ethel and the children were appalled at what they saw, an apparently abandoned horse, miserable and starving, dehydrated to mere "skin and bones." A feed bucket was in the shack, but a neck halter restrained the horse. The distraught animal had thrashed a hole in the floor trying to reach the bucket.

Ethel raced home with the children and asked her groom, Richard Mayberry, to go rescue the horse and bring it to Hickory Hill, which he promptly did. She called the Animal Welfare League of Fairfax County. It sent over an agent and launched an investigation that turned up six more distressed horses on Zemo's farm.

Mayberry and the Kennedys' veterinarian worked day and night, but the poor horse was too far gone. After five days of intensive ministrations at Hickory Hill, it died.

Ethel was furious. At her urging, the league filed charges against Zemo. She testified as principal witness and enjoyed a new celebrity as "the Good Samaritan on horseback." Zemo was convicted on November 7, 1963, of cruelty to animals, fined $250 and given a suspended six-month jail sentence. County Judge William G. Plummer called it "one of the clearest cases of cruelty by neglect I have ever seen."

The only good thing that came of it for Zemo was the return of his six other horses, after the League restored their health and he promised to take better care of them.

Still, Zemo wanted revenge. On October 7, 1965, he brought the civil suit against Ethel, charging that the horse she had caused Mayberry to take from his farm was a thoroughbred yearling named Pande that died while at Hickory Hill illegally on October 13, 1963.

Attorneys Oberdorfer and Williams went for the jugular.

They sought to tell the seven-man jury about Zemo's 1963 conviction for cruelty to animals, to contrast that with Ethel's altruistic role as a Florence Nightingale "not afraid to become involved." They even cited the recent case of New York's Kitty Genovese, beaten to death in her apartment complex while neighbors ignored her cries for help. Judge Albert V. Bryan, Jr., would not let them show evidence of cruelty at first, but he later relented.

Oberdorfer and Williams attacked with the preparation and resourcefulness that Bob's Justice Department had brought to prosecuting its labor-racketeering case against James Hoffa. They brought in a battery of expert witnesses.

One said the horse, even if healthy and a thoroughbred, was worth "less than a thousand dollars" and not the thirty thousand dollars that Zemo claimed. Four others testified that the horse they saw at Hickory Hill was not the same yearling named Pande described on his American Jockey Club registration certificate. The same four said they saw no injury on the horse's leg that might have caused him to quit eating, as Zemo argued. And the veterinarian said the horse was so near death when he examined him at Hickory Hill as to be worthless.

Zemo had submitted photographs of the horse that, he said, showed it was healthy two or three days before Ethel found him. Oberdorfer introduced a meteorologist who testified that the length of shadows in the pictures proved they were taken several months earlier than October. He said such shadow-measuring, used in analyzing aerial-reconnaissance work over Cuba and Vietnam, was precise and irrefutable.

When Ethel took the stand, Zemo's attorney, Martin E. Morris, maneuvered her into saying she did not actually see the dead horse. How, then, could she swear he had died? Ethel flared back, with a logic that seemed straight out of Manhattanville: "How do you know Europe's over there?" Morris told her testily that he was the one asking the questions and she was the one answering them. She fixed him with her trademark glare but held her tongue.

In his summation, Morris brushed aside the Good Samaritan metaphor that Oberdorfer had embraced. He said that, however well intentioned Ethel was, the fact remained that she had stubbornly ignored Zemo's property rights and had gone out of her way to vent her anger at him.

"If we were all allowed to do what we think is right without considering property rights, then we might as well do away with the law," Morris argued. As to Ethel's temper, he told jurors:

"She took it upon herself to get angry with him. You've all seen Mrs. Kennedy on the witness stand. She got angry with me."

The jury was out for two and a half hours. When it returned, there was a standing-room-only crowd of about seventy-five persons, almost all friends and supporters of Ethel, who wore an off-white maternity outfit for the occasion. Assistant court clerk Edward Young read the verdict:

"We find for the defendant."

Ethel gave a little yelp. Beaming, she shook hands all around. She went quickly to another room and telephoned Bob, who was waiting for the verdict at his Senate office. Outside, she got her customary stage fright under control and faced the television cameras. She would do it all over any time, because "I don't think I could live with myself if I didn't."

Asked what her husband had to say, she sighed:

"I don't think he's going to let me off the property again."

17

The Coatimundi

While more U.S. forces moved into Vietnam, racial tensions deepened on the home front. By the end of 1967, there were 475,000 U.S. troops in South Vietnam, and all of North Vietnam was being bombed. Antiwar protests began springing up across America while the civil rights front seethed. In Newark, New Jersey, black riots killed 26 and injured 1,500, with more than 1,000 arrested. In Detroit, 4,700 U.S. Army paratroopers and 8,000 National Guardsmen put down black ghetto rioting, looting and burning that killed 40, injured 2,000 and left 5,000 homeless. The Middle East erupted in a brief, costly war, with Israel triumphant over its Arab neighbors and becoming a stronger presence in the area. In Congress, Democratic Rep. Adam Clayton Powell of New York, a black, was denied his House seat for financial irregularities (reelected in 1968, he was seated again but with the loss of twenty-two years' seniority). Republican Edward Brooke of Massachusetts won election to the U.S. Senate as its first black in eighty-five years. Democrats Carl B. Stokes of Cleveland and Richard G. Hatcher of Gary, Indiana, were elected the first black mayors of major U.S. cities. Thurgood Marshall was sworn in as the first black Supreme Court justice. President Johnson met with Soviet Premier Aleksei Kosygin at Glassboro State College in New Jersey seeking peaceful accord. Bob Kennedy talked, inconclusively, with North Vietnamese in Paris about a peace settlement. He reported to President Johnson, urging a halt in the bombing as a prelude to a peace settlement. Rebuffed, he prepared to make a public break, working long hours on the issue with aides, often at Hickory Hill.

Bob and Ethel tolerated young Bobby's taste in bizarre animals, having encouraged him with a terrarium and even an elaborate system of cages in the basement, plus plenty of space in the barn. Nobody in the family raised an eyebrow as he moved in snakes and iguanas, hawks and falcons, dwarf ponies smaller than Brumus, a honey bear that slept in bookcases by day and raided the refrigerator by night, baby pigs with wanderlust, a seal named Sandy that lived in the swimming pool until banished to the zoo as an incorrigible escapee, and more. But St. Francis himself might have had misgivings about Bobby's coatimundi.

Ethel certainly looked askance at the feisty, South American cousin of a raccoon, distinguished by its skinny, flexible snout and long ringed tail. Sharp claws and teeth complemented a hostile glare. Young Bobby had a knack with animals, she knew, but he was a long way from controlling this one. Soon after it arrived, it broke away and, when Bobby tried to capture it, he came under ferocious attack. It leaped over a couch and chased Bobby all around the basement until, with help, he cornered and subdued it, still fighting.

The coatimundi's last day at Hickory Hill would have been a momentous one without the spectacular manner of its departure. It was March 2, 1967, and the house had been in turmoil for days over a speech that Bob was preparing to deliver in the Senate that afternoon. It marked his formal break with the Vietnam War policies of President Lyndon B. Johnson and called for a bombing halt as a prelude to a negotiated settlement. He had been working through most of the night with speechwriters and typists at his home, revising and cutting and adding, and, when the day dawned, they were still at it.

But real life went on at Hickory Hill. As with every day,

breakfast time was the children's hour. Writer and television commentator Dick Schaap, who was there interviewing Bob and Ethel for his book, *R.F.K.*, took in the scene with wonder: Thirteen-year-old Bobby and eleven-year-old David, howling with laughter, kicked a basketball around the hallway like a soccer ball, pursued by eight-year-old Michael. Christopher, three, and Max, two, fought noisily over leftover party balloons in the little den. Brumus bounded about, but Freckles and another dog named Battle Star stayed out of the traffic. So did Courtney, ten, busy collecting her notebooks. Kerry, seven, lay upstairs with a cold. Kathleen, fifteen, and Joe, fourteen, were away at school.

Maids carried coffee and eggs upstairs to Bob's staff people, still pounding away at the speech. Bob came down, hair askew, unshaven, bleary-eyed, hunched inside a blue dressing gown. Ethel, just three weeks away from giving birth to Douglas, sat at the dining table in a purple maternity dress. She motioned Bob to his waiting poached eggs and bacon, giggled and greeted him above the din:

"Hail, Caesar!"

Schaap noticed Bob's hands trembling as he picked up the bacon with his fingers. Indeed, he was acutely shy, which few people knew, and his hands always shook when he was under stress or anticipated stress. Speaking in public was a special ordeal for him. He could do it but he could not control the shakes. He knew he had a controversial speech this time, one certain to divide the Senate and the Democrats further on the war.

"I spoke to Teddy last night," he told Ethel. "He said to make sure that they announce it's the Kennedy from New York."

And then he added:

"A lot of people think I'm out of my mind. You could almost get a unanimous opinion on that."

He went upstairs to bathe and dress. Ethel picked that as a good time to give Schaap a guided tour of young Bobby's animal world in the basement. She was most excited about his latest acquisition, the coatimundi.

Ethel took the little fellow out of his cage and petted him. She put him on the floor and he pawed gently at Schaap's pants leg. Ethel moved toward the cages where Bobby kept his snakes, iguanas and other reptiles. Suddenly, the coatimundi sprang at Ethel, digging into her legs with teeth and claws, biting and scratching.

"Get him off me!" she screamed. "Get him off me! Oh, God, he's biting me!"

Schaap lifted her to the top of a wooden cabinet. She shook violently and he swatted at the animal until, finally, it let go. He kicked at it and it ran out through an open door. Ethel, her legs scratched and bleeding, trembled uncontrollably and kept saying, "I'm so sorry."

Sue Markham, an old friend, heard the ruckus and entered the basement by the backdoor. To Schaap's astonishment, Ethel pulled herself together and, with a correctness that would have pleased the nuns at Manhattanville, made the introduction:

"Sue Markham, this is Dick Schaap. Dick, this is Sue Markham."

She started shaking again and gasping for air. She got down from the cabinet and limped off with Sue, who drove her to a nearby doctor. A veterinarian was summoned to deal with the coatimundi, locked up by then in a basement storeroom. Ethel returned, legs bandaged and daubed with antiseptic, just as Bob was setting out to make his speech and the vet was carting off her nemesis.

Like a Marx Brothers movie, a horse van with Sargent Shriver's name on it pulled into the driveway just then and began unloading tables and chairs. The Kennedy brother-in-law, husband of Eunice, had borrowed them for a party the night before.

Ethel waved goodbye to the coatimundi and teased her husband:

"If these are all the scars the Kennedys end up with by five o'clock, it'll be all right."

It was almost four o'clock before Bob rose to speak and half past six when the Senate debate ended. Ethel was there, in the family gallery, bandages and all.

18

California

America's political scene was in turmoil as 1968 began. Protests against the Vietnam War split the country. In the Sea of Japan, North Koreans seized the USS Pueblo and held its eighty-three man crew for a year. In South Vietnam, a Communist offensive on the Tet holiday swept into Saigon, even into the U.S. Embassy. It was a Pyrrhic victory, in that it destroyed the Vietcong as a fighting force, but its impact on American public opinion was so adverse that U.S. withdrawal was inevitable. President Johnson began reducing the bombing in North Vietnam. Peace talks began in Paris. In Memphis, Tennessee, escaped convict James Earl Ray shot and killed civil rights leader Martin Luther King, Jr., the 1964 Nobel Laureate for Peace. President Johnson decided it would be too divisive for the country if he ran for reelection, and Bob Kennedy, with his most implacable foe out of the race, saw a chance to win the Democratic nomination despite early leads by Vice President Hubert H. Humphrey and Minnesota Senator Eugene J. McCarthy.

Ethel Kennedy had seemed to be enjoying that election night in California more than any other politicking she had ever done with Bob. She had been out on the campaign trail before, when Bob had managed his brother John's successful bids for the House, the Senate and the Presidency, but only a few times and in a minor role. She had done a little too, when Bob ran for and won his Senate seat in 1964, but it was not until the Indiana primary in 1968 really that she appeared to be getting into the swing of things as "the candidate's wife." Only then did she seem to be enjoying herself in the role. Up front and in the limelight was not where she was most comfortable. Supporting Bob Kennedy in whatever he did was the only public role for her, that and their children. Sometimes, the support was literal, as Bob noted in his 1962 book, *Just Friends and Brave Enemies*, published by Harper & Row. He dedicated the book to his parents and to Ethel, citing the pledge of Ruth 1:16–17 in the Bible:

> And Ruth said . . .
> Whither thou goest, I will go;
> And where thou lodgest, I will lodge;
> Thy people shall be my people,
> And thy God my God;
> Where thou diest, will I die,
> And there will I be buried;
> Jehovah do so to me, and more also,
> If ought but death part thee and me.

Bob told in *Just Friends and Brave Enemies* about his 1962 world tour with Ethel. One highlight was a near-impromptu speech before 160,000 shivering West Berliners at City Hall Square. He and Ethel had just arrived from the warmer climate of Rome that February 22. He had not expected to be making his speech outdoors, but protocol required it. He worked up some notes and pitched in. As he recalled the event:

> I had trouble beginning my speech—I was so cold I had difficulty saying the first words. I had just come from an extremely warm climate and had not adjusted to the freezing weather. Further, I had lost my overcoat in Hong Kong . . . So, as I stood up in front of that vast multitude of people, I was shaking so hard that speaking was

extremely difficult. Ethel saved the day by coming up behind me and unobtrusively rubbing my back, which gave me enough warmth to get through the short speech.

Ethel was in California backing him up too, six years later. He had just lost the 1968 Oregon primary—the first Kennedy to lose an election—and it was make or break in California. If he was ever to overtake the front-runner, Vice President Hubert H. Humphrey, in that chaotic 1968 campaign for the Democratic presidential nomination, he would have to win in California. Exhausted to the point of nausea, Bob nevertheless pushed on, driving himself almost to collapse.

Only the day before—on the final day of campaigning before the voting on Tuesday—he had become so sick to his stomach while speaking in San Diego that he had had to stop, go offstage for a while and clear his head. He tried to vomit, but he could not. Still, he went back to the rostrum, apologized to the audience for the interruption, and finished the speech.

That night, Bob and Ethel and six of their children moved into the Malibu Beach home of the movie director, John Frankenheimer, and the next day, Election Day, with nothing more he could do to influence the voters, Bob gave himself over to pure relaxation, at least until the evening, when the returns began coming in. Still, tension stalked Bob. In between stretching out by Frankenheimer's pool and splashing in the Pacific Ocean surf with his children, he had to dive into the sea at one point and rescue his son David. Dazed from a knock on the head when a wave slapped him down, David was being carried away by a strong undertow just as Bob got to him.

In the evening, as Frankenheimer drove him rather speedily toward the Ambassador Hotel on the Santa Monica Freeway, Bob cautioned, "Take it easy, John . . . Life is too short . . . "

In the Kennedy campaign suite, 516, at the Ambassador, the air was festive. More so than on most other such election nights, there was cause for optimism. Kennedy had beaten his chief opponent, Eugene McCarthy, in their televised debate, the polls indicated, and there was every reason to believe he could reverse and erase McCarthy's victory over him in the May 28 Oregon primary (44.7 percent to 38.8 percent). Democratic Senator George S. McGovern, a staunch Kennedy worker, had called from South Dakota to report victory in his state (46.3 percent for Kennedy, 41.8 percent for McCarthy), and Bob and his top people hoped that McCarthy's ranks might crumble, with people like John Kenneth Galbraith and Allard Lowenstein ready to come over to Kennedy if he won big in California. After that, it was on to New York for another must-win primary in the state that Kennedy represented in the United States Senate, the possibility of arranging a primary in Rhode Island in July as a challenge to Humphrey, and intensive personal campaigning by Kennedy in the nonprimary states that he had neglected because of his late entry into the race and his concentration, of necessity, on the primaries.

The Kennedy campaign suite was huge. It was supposed to be for family and close friends only, but it was jammed from wall to wall. Several big television sets were blaring out election returns pointing to a Kennedy victory. People of all ages, some of them Kennedys, some staffers and some like me, with a professional interest in the proceedings, looked at the TV sets, talked to each other in blithe disregard of their electronic babble, or kept an eye on little children who tumbled and collapsed in giggles on the carpet amid soft drink bottles and paper cups and stacks of campaign literature.

Here and there were clusters of the political news sources we had been dealing with during Bob's pell-mell, eighty-day campaign for the Democratic presidential nomination, and of other political reporters like myself (I was then Washington editor of *LOOK* magazine) as well as *LOOK* photographer Stanley Tretick. I nodded and waved acknowledgments to them all when our eyes met—Jimmy Breslin, Hays Gorey, Pete Hamill, Richard Harwood, Jack Newfield, George Plimpton, Loudon Wainwright, Theodore White and a whole lot more. Telephones kept jangling and whoever was nearby would answer them, sometimes a Kennedy or one of us but often one of the toddlers barely able to say, "Hu'wo?" I had the distinct feeling that I had wandered into a Federico Fellini movie just as it began to soar to its fullest heights, all action and no meaning.

Across the hall on that madcap fifth floor was the candidate's private suite, 511, consisting of a bedroom, a bath and a sitting room. Bob and Ethel were there getting dressed for the planned victory celebration in the Ambassador's Embassy Ballroom downstairs. I knocked on the door, and I heard Bob's, "Who is it?" I identified myself. He said, "Come in," and I did.

Arthur M. Schlesinger, Jr., in his definitive book, *Robert Kennedy and His Times*, published by Houghton Mifflin Company in 1978, has written of how Bob Kennedy seemed to draw journalists into whatever he was doing. Schlesinger quoted Jules Witcover, who wrote beautifully of Bob's relationships with people close to him in *85 Days: The Last Campaign of Robert Kennedy*, published by G. P. Putnam's Sons in 1969, as noting Kennedy's "way of pulling individuals around him into his orbit, a strange disarming quality about him that somehow evoked sympathy."

Stan Tretick and I felt that too over the years we had been covering Bob as his brother's campaign manager, counsel to congressional investigators, Attorney General, United States Senator and candidate for the Democratic presidential nomination. In the 1968 campaign, we had a more special reason for staying closer to him than would otherwise have been the case. We had been assigned by *LOOK* magazine to do an intimate, detailed study of precisely how Bob pursued his campaign.

To do that, we needed a kind of close cooperation that no journalists had ever enjoyed from any politician, as far as we knew, and that included Teddy White and his 1960 arrangement with Jack Kennedy, for we were talking about carte blanche on photographic as well as reportorial access. And yet, typically, Bob gave me the promise of full cooperation on both counts almost before I finished explaining the proposition: We wanted to walk lockstep with him through the campaign, as if we were members of his staff, going everywhere, seeing and hearing everything, with nothing held back, and he would trust our discretion to honor all legitimate confidences.

The idea was that *LOOK* would do in pictures as well as in words what Teddy White had done so brilliantly with Jack Kennedy in 1960—that is, to tell the story of a presidential campaign from the inside out. Bob had caught the significance immediately: For the first time, there would be a graphic history in words *and* pictures of what it was like—really like—to run for and achieve the presidency, from Hamlet-like backings and fillings at the outset to the self-assured, resolute drive to victory that all of those involved anticipated at the end.

I had the added conviction that, if Bob did not make it, we would always go with the story as depicting the end of the Kennedy dynasty, or something like that. Bob and I never discussed that sort of story with its unhappy ending. But I do not think it would have made any difference to him that I was prepared to write it if he failed. He still would have seen its value as journalism and history. And the suggestion might have provoked a lively discussion with him about what could go wrong and how he might avoid that.

As a result of our agreement, I was used to going into the candidate's room at the end of his day in public. I had been covering national politics at that point for eighteen years and Louisiana politics for four years before that. I thought I had learned most of the tricks of the trade. I felt I had a handle on what made politics work and what made politicians tick. But it was not until that 1968 campaign of Bob Kennedy's, when I had freedom to move about his campaign headquarters virtually without restriction, that I began to understand how the thing was put together and what made it go.

Until then, as with the other political reporters, at the end of the day I would see the candidate safely into his headquarters suite, watch the door close behind him and then go on about my own business of filing the day's report, having dinner and bedding down for a quick night's sleep until campaigning began again the next day, usually at the crack of dawn, with a bouncing ride over bad roads in a weakly sprung bus.

Bob looked extremely tired as he greeted me at the door of Suite 511, puffy-eyed and hollow-cheeked. He had slept late that day in Malibu and, in between swims (and rescuing son David from drowning), had napped, so the look of fatigue was the bone-deep exhaustion left over from the Oregon and California campaigns, too much for one day of rest and relaxation to overcome. He told me he felt fine when I inquired about his health. I knew it was his stock answer. He looked worn out.

"Have you heard about the Indian vote?" he asked. He was fumbling with a cuff link, a ritual I had observed many times on the campaign trail, and his hair was wet from the shower and not yet combed. He had already given three interviews—to Roger Mudd for CBS television, Bob Clark for ABC television and Dan Blackburn for Metromedia radio—and the last big event, before a staff and press celebration at Pierre Salinger's jet set discotheque, the Factory, was a formal victory statement in the Embassy Ballroom downstairs. "You know that Indian precinct in South Dakota we were watching? We got eight hundred and seventy-eight votes and Humphrey got nine. McCarthy got two."

Ethel, fully dressed and seemingly ready to go, relaxed on the bed, out of the way as Bob ranged around the room, getting himself together. She waved a hello and listened too, as I told Bob I had Budd Schulberg and his wife, the actress Geraldine Brooks, with me, waiting in the hall outside, and Budd wanted a few minutes to bring him up to date on the Watts Writers Workshop. Budd had gone into that Los Angeles ghetto immediately after the 1965 riots there, as had many other Hollywood celebrities, to heed the residents' calls for help. The difference with Budd was that the others left when the television cameras left and he stayed on. Some of the young black writers he helped train stayed in the craft, making it a career, and at least one of them won an Emmy Award for a television script that Budd's brother Stuart produced for NBC. Budd, widely respected for his classic novel, *What Makes Sammy Run?*, and his Oscar-winning screenplay, *On the Waterfront*, later helped start a similar workshop in New York City, the Frederick Douglass Creative Arts Center.

Budd and Bob had worked closely on Schulberg's adaptation of Kennedy's book, *The Enemy Within*, hailed by all who read it as a masterful screenplay although it was never made into a movie. Bob's book was a factual account of labor racketeering, built specifically around the investigations he led that eventually jailed Teamsters Union President James R. Hoffa. Budd's screenplay was a fictionalized version, with the Hoffa-like character deteriorating from a two-fisted man of the people to a double-dealing, racketeering labor overlord. Threats of union boycotts, and worse, destroyed all chance of having the script produced for years until, as the movie market changed, interest in the idea waned (although Sylvester Stallone later produced what looked like a clone called *F.I.S.T.*). Their collaboration bonded Budd and Bob and, like the rest of us, Budd believed in Bob and was ready to do whatever he could to work with him to ease the lot of the poor, the minorities and all other hard-luck Americans whom Bob had chosen as his constituency.

The point with people like Schulberg, who would be doing what they did with or without Bob Kennedy, was that Bob was the only person in public life at that time to whom they would risk turning. He was the only one who offered them credible hope of a consistent attempt to make things better for people who had nothing at all, or next to it.

"Sure," Bob said, "why don't you take him into the next room. A lot of people you know are in there." And then, as I acted on this gentle shooing-out, he added, more to Ethel than to me, "Budd worked hard for us in the California campaign. He's a good man."

Budd and his wife Gerry and I rejoined the others across

the hall for a few minutes, and then we went back to Bob and Ethel's suite, the sitting-room part of it this time. Bob was quite different. He had shed the fatigue, and he appeared all pumped up by his own excitement. He had virtually challenged Vice President Hubert H. Humphrey to meet him in debate over the key issues in the campaign. This was the linchpin of his strategy, for, with McCarthy effectively neutralized, his next move had to be to go after Humphrey, all out. He had just beaten Humphrey in the state where he was born, South Dakota, and he had done it on the same day that he had overcome the Oregon defeat by knocking off McCarthy in California (but just barely, as final returns later showed).

Now, Bob was pacing the room like a caged panther. For a while, he would sit on his haunches in a corner, scrunched into the angle of the walls and floor like a child being punished, and the people there, all close friends, would go to him one or two at a time, bend over and chat. And then he would bound up, holding his victory cigar at an awkward, unpracticed angle. He would prowl in circles around the room, punching a fist into a palm and announcing, to no one in particular, over and over:

"I'm going to get Humphrey! I'm going to *make* him debate me! I'm going to chase his ass all around the country, and I'm going to *make* him debate me!"

For Bob, that was uncharacteristically rough language. I had never heard him use a word like "ass" in a large group before. Nor had I ever heard him so publicly (more or less) disrespectful of Humphrey, whom he truly liked. It struck me that his excitement might have indicated some uncertainty about how he was to cope with the enormous tasks that still lay ahead. He had to win the primary the following week in New York, where he was very much the underdog even though he represented the state in the United States Senate. And then he had to try to draw Humphrey into a Rhode Island primary in July—a one-on-one confrontation that he probably could win—if a petition being circulated could bring about such voting.

Beyond that, he had to try to wrest from Humphrey whatever support the Vice President had accumulated in the big industrial states that had no primaries. If all this was to be done, and it had to be, or there was no chance for the nomination at the convention in Chicago, it had to be done by Bob himself. No surrogates would serve, and he knew it. The wise money (including a lot of the political reporters sharing his hospitality that night) would have bet against his pulling off such a political miracle.

I had thought, along with others, that Bob had foredoomed his chances by allowing McCarthy to step out as point man against President Lyndon B. Johnson and by then jumping in himself only after McCarthy dramatized Johnson's vulnerability in the New Hampshire primary. I felt that, given McCarthy's attitude that Bob had betrayed him politically by his late entry, plus the personal dislike that was mutual, together with some good old Irish vindictiveness, there was no way that Bob could rally the forces divided between them in time to head off heir-apparent Humphrey at the pass. Johnson's unequivocal withdrawal, moreover, had seemed to ensure Humphrey overwhelming superiority in the convention's delegate counts up to then.

I had laid all this out to Bob one midnight in a virtually empty restaurant in the Midwest, over a late supper with him and photographer Tretick, my colleague at *LOOK*, along with a half-dozen or so campaign staffers and "Bob's astronaut," John Glenn. I was the only one there, the discussion disclosed, who felt the candidate was going to fall short. I was taken aback at how gravely Bob took this. The corners of his mouth turned down, and he stared at his hands, upturned and motionless on his lap, a posture of passivity he often struck when he was very tired and appearing most vulnerable.

After a silence, he sighed and said softly, "I can't believe that, all our work for nothing." And he launched into an argument built around a strategy that consisted mainly of uniting McCarthy's people behind him for a frontal assault on the

Democratic establishment. Aggressiveness was the key, plus unceasing pressure on the opposition. It was a blueprint for a blitz.

On that fateful night in California, with twin victories assured in South Dakota and California, and with possibilities opening up in New York and elsewhere, Bob's campaign seemed to be reaching a new plateau. For the first time, he looked to me like a possibility, perhaps even a probability. And I was confident that, if he won the nomination, he was Kennedy enough to spook the Republicans' certain candidate, Richard M. Nixon, just as his brother Jack had in 1960. More than any other leading figure in either major party, Bob understood the pressures for social change that were sweeping the country in the late 1960s, and he was demonstrating he could translate that understanding into public support in the voting booth.

It seemed important to me that night to tell Bob that. And I did, just after he had slammed a fist into a palm for the third or fourth time and pledged to chase Humphrey across the land until he cornered him in a debate.

"For what it's worth," I heard myself saying, "I think you can do it now. I didn't before, but I do now. I think you can beat Humphrey and get the nomination."

He studied me for a couple of seconds and then broke into a grin. "Glad to have your endorsement, at last," he said, wryly. "Welcome aboard the bandwagon."

Kennedy and Schulberg were in an earnest discussion, amid all the hubbub of others talking and laughing in the sitting room, when Jesse "Big Daddy" Unruh, speaker of the California assembly and a major force for Kennedy in the state, began tugging at Bob's elbow.

"Time to go, Bob," he said, gently.

I surveyed his bulk and my right elbow throbbed with remembered pain. Earlier, Unruh had nearly broken my arm. Left behind when the candidate's convertible suddenly departed a handshaking stop, he had run pell-mell, leaped high and landed his considerable bottom atop the open car's rear door. My arm was there, gripping the door to balance the pull of Bill Barry as I reached back to steady him. It was our usual posture on the road: Bob standing on the rear of the car inside a screen provided by Bill's chest and crooked arm as he knelt on the trunk and, with his free hand, held tight to my hand as I sat as rigidly as I could inside the car.

"Boy, you got some arm!" Bill would grin after he had hopped into the backseat as we sped away. It was not true. Mine was the easy job. He was the one with the arm and with the courage and fortitude to make it work.

Crowds had pulled Bob off the back of the convertible when others were doing Bill's kneeling-and-screening number. After Bill took over the task permanently, he had pulled a few others out of the car seat until I took over. The physical side of political campaigning is a book by itself.

After Unruh bottomed out on my arm, it was purple for weeks, shoulder to elbow, and Unruh, a courteous man, repeatedly inquired solicitously about its condition. For years afterward, whenever we met, he would ask, "How's the arm?"

Unruh led the way to the elevator. Bob was detained by well-wishers in the hallway, and another big man, Roosevelt Grier, quietly urged him on. "Time to go, eh?" Bob asked, and Rosey nodded and flashed his little boy's grin. Bob was intrigued with the civility of this gentle giant, as against the ferocity with which he played defensive tackle for the Los Angeles Rams, and with the three-hundred-pounds-plus size of him. Once, backstage during a charity telethon in Washington, D.C., Bob clownishly began climbing Rosey, as if going up a mountain. Bob silently and elaborately demonstrated techniques he had learned from Jim Whittaker when they scaled Mount Kennedy in the Yukon. It was all in exquisite pantomime, with Bob mock-grimly dragging himself up Rosey's side, resting awhile and then plodding on to his shoulders and neck, and finally planting himself triumphantly astride Rosey's shoulders. All the time, Rosey simply braced, saying nothing but grinning broadly, ever the gentle giant.

There was a traffic jam at the elevator, the usual thing in any campaign when the candidate is on the move. Budd and Gerry Schulberg and I managed to squeeze in with Bob and Ethel, along with Barry, who had been an FBI agent and was Bob's only security man and who always walked just ahead of him in crowds, and Rafer Johnson, the tall and elegant Olympic decathlon champion, as well as Unruh, Grier, and Frederick G. Dutton, Bob's politically clever and personally devoted campaign manager (only a couple of days earlier I had seen Fred padding around at a campaign stop in his stocking feet, and he had explained, "Somebody pulled the candidate's shoes off him and I gave him mine"), plus a few other triumphant celebrants. Not everybody in the hall who wanted to could fit into the elevator. Kennedy was distressed that he could not find Cesar Chavez, the leader of the Mexican-American farm workers in California, to stand with him on the podium when he made his victory statement. They had been close friends and political allies for years.

The Embassy Ballroom was rocking with a party roaring toward a climax. A great shout went up when the crowd spotted the Kennedys and it continued until Bob took over the small platform's microphone from his brother-in-law, Steve Smith, husband of Jean, who had been "filling" for him with the crowd. Rollicking cheers punctuated Bob's lighthearted, self-deprecating speech.

He thanked just about everybody, including "my dog Freckles—I'm not doing this in the order of importance—I also want to thank my wife, Ethel," and he gave special attention to students, blacks and Chicanos who had worked for his California victory. He pledged once more to try to get Humphrey to debate the issues with him, and he ended with a two-fingered V-for-Victory sign and a cry of "Let's win!" The crowd signaled back and took up a "We Want Kennedy!" chant as it swarmed around him.

"Take care of Ethel," Bob said to Barry.

Bill hesitated. He felt his place was directly in front of Bob, where he had been throughout the eighty days of the campaign. He was worried about possible injury among the squirming, shoving, shouting celebrants despite all their good wishes. But he knew, as few others did, that Ethel was pregnant again (with Rory Elizabeth Katherine, the Kennedys' eleventh child and fourth daughter, born the following December 12). Bill found another Kennedy staffer to help Ethel through the crowd and began pushing his way back toward Bob.

Budd and Gerry Schulberg and I, joined in the ballroom by Richard Harwood of the *Washington Post*, had made our way to the lobby outside as Bob talked. We then went to the Colonial Room, a smaller conference facility next door to the ballroom. It was the same route that Bob was due to take to meet us there. I had told him that the "writing press" was demanding equal time with television. Charles W. Bailey II of the *Des Moines Register*, William Theis of Hearst Newspapers and a half-dozen other Washington-based correspondents covering the campaign had asked me to get the candidate to meet with us "pencil types" immediately after his televised victory statement and before he went on to the victory party at Salinger's club, the Factory. They felt entitled to a question-and-answer session like Bob's with ABC, CBS, and Metromedia, and Bob laughingly agreed they had a point.

Bob was on his way to us in the Colonial Room to keep his date, but a particularly boisterous batch of well-wishers shouting, "Bobby! Bobby! Bobby!," blocked his path to the exit from the ballroom. Instead of following Dutton, who was clearing a route, Bob let himself be shunted in the opposite direction by Karl Uecker, assistant maître d'hôtel of the Ambassador, toward the tunnel-like kitchen area that offered a short-cut, connecting the ballroom and the Colonial Room. Dutton and Barry seeing this shifted direction themselves, but it was rough going through the happy crowd.

In the Colonial Room, we watched the scene on closed-circuit television. My colleagues began taking their seats and preparing their notebooks and ballpoint pens. Some were still riding me about how long it was taking Bob to get to them, suggesting it was somehow my fault. "Where the hell is he?" somebody griped. The TV camera had lost him, apparently, as he made his way into the kitchen from the ballroom. I decided to go get him and lead him in. That would give me something to do and take me away from my colleagues' needling.

At the metal-covered, double swinging doors leading to the kitchen, Bill Theis called out to me. I hesitated and turned to him, more out of politeness than interest, because like everybody else I wanted to get on with the interview and head for the party at Salinger's club.

"Let me tell you about a funny thing that happened to me a little while ago," Bill began.

I listened but not too attentively, and I edged around him toward the doors, hoping he would follow while talking and we could look inside to see how far away Bob was at the other end of the kitchen corridor.

It was then I heard the shots.

19

"Gently, gently . . ."

Minnesota Senator Eugene J. McCarthy beat Robert Kennedy, 44.7 percent to 38.8 percent in the Oregon primary, the first election lost by a Kennedy, except for the Harvard Board of Overseers. In California, Kennedy reversed that, not by much, but enough to convince him he could go all the way. That was what he was prepared to say as he made his way through the Ambassador Hotel kitchen to the Colonial Room, where newspaper and magazine correspondents covering his campaign (the "writing press," as opposed to omnivorous, omnipotent television) waited, watching his ballroom victory statement and his movement toward them on a TV monitor.

They sounded like firecrackers. I remember thinking at the time that whenever I heard gunshots, they always sounded like firecrackers, and I wondered why they always sounded like firecrackers.

There were eight shots in rapid succession. But to me it sounded like only four: *Pop!* A one-second pause. And then, *Pop! Pop! Pop!*

I thought, "What a stupid, tasteless way to celebrate!"

But in the next split second, I was running through the swinging doors.

Out of the corner of my eye, to the left, I saw little Gerry Schulberg, five foot two and about a hundred pounds, go sailing into the wall. I realized she had dashed into the kitchen corridor alongside me, just in time to get swatted away by a flying elbow from me as I ran ahead of her.

I banged into a wave of people, mostly young girls screaming, "He's shot! He's shot! Get a doctor!"

And then I crashed into a tight knot of men, a half-dozen or so, all twisted together like some pretzelized freak of a sideshow animal.

At once I was part of it. There were people pressing me into the melee from behind and people clutching from both sides. I could recognize some. Rosey. Rafer. Bill Barry. Dun Gifford and George Plimpton, both also closely connected with the campaign. My cheek pressed hard against somebody's face. The man was going, "Yuk, yuk, yuk!" There was an arm around his neck—Rosey's, I believe—and another arm around his head—perhaps Barry's. Our cheeks jammed harder together, my eye against his eye, and his was wild and glistening. This was the assailant, the Jordanian named Sirhan Bishara Sirhan.

In those first few seconds, as I held on to him, struggling in the pack to stay on my feet, I clung to his right leg, clad in pale-blue denim and lifted completely off the floor. I pulled back in the crush for a better look at him. I saw in a flash that he had a swarthy complexion and black curly hair, and I had a terrible sinking feeling as I thought:

"My God, he looks like a Mexican! Oh, Bob! Oh, Cesar! After all you've done! Shot down by a Mexican!"

We staggered around, that great bunch of us, like a football scrimmage, a goal-line stand. As in football, there was pushing and punching and a good deal of yelling. "Get the gun! Get the gun! Kill him! No, don't hurt him! Kill him! Break his thumb! No! No! We don't want another Dallas here!"

Protruding from the pack, incredibly, was an arm, the left arm of the assailant, and it ended in a hand grasping, not a football, but a pistol. It was small, a .22-caliber, snub-nosed revolver, and I could not comprehend how that little man, hardly more than five feet tall and a slender 125 pounds or so, could continue to hold on to it. Hands clutched his arm, some white and some black, like the famous photograph of white and black workmen's hands cooperatively tugging a huge wrench in Edward Steichen's *Family of Man* collection.

As we banged into the kitchen's stainless steel steam table, I saw Rafer Johnson trying to peel Sirhan's fingers from the butt of the pistol. He looked studied and precise, as if he were stripping away the leaves of an artichoke in some televised parlor game. A man jumped up on the steam table and kicked at the pistol, which did not make Rafer's efforts go any easier. Then somebody in the pack started a rocking motion that kept slamming Sirhan's hand and the pistol on the top of the steam table. This made a loud and rhythmic noise, but the weapon still refused to come loose.

Bill Barry, especially, was determined to get the pistol. He had taken it away from Sirhan just seconds after he fired, chopping him across the wrist and twisting it out of his fist. He had subdued him with a couple of punches and a stranglehold. But he wanted to go to Bob, and so he handed Sirhan over to Rosey Grier and Jack Gallivan, saying, "Take this guy. Get this guy off in a corner where people can't hit him." But Rosey was in a state of shock. For all his power and agility on the football field, the big man could not hold on to little Sirhan, who squiggled out of his grasp and away from Gallivan too, and picked the revolver up from the steam table where Bill had put it.

Barry went to Bob, took off his suit jacket and put it under his head. But he saw Rosey and the rest of us struggling with Sirhan and the pistol—which we all thought was still partly loaded—and he jumped back into the mixup.

Everything seemed in slow motion, as it always does for me in crises of this sort. And in that state, it soon hit me that I did not belong in that pack of people. I am six feet tall, but, except for Sirhan, everybody was bigger and stronger. And there were more than enough, perhaps too many. Besides, as a reporter, my job was observing, not participating.

I let go of Sirhan's leg and jumped up on the steam table. I knelt to get a better view. A man already on the steam table, in white cotton shirt and trousers that suggested he worked in the kitchen, was screaming at the assailant. He shouted hysterically over and over:

"You filthy monster! You're going to die for this! Why did you do it? You're going to die, you hear me? You're going to die!"

I leaned toward him and, in as cold and curt and quiet a voice as I could muster, commanded:

"Shut up!"

He did. He looked surprised, but he shut up, as if I had suddenly pulled his plug.

I looked down and saw at last, at agonizingly long last, the fingers slowly uncurling from the pistol. Rafer Johnson held the weapon in his big hand, staring down at it as if unable to comprehend its existence. The others, carrying Sirhan spread-eagled, hustled him out through the swinging doors into the Colonial Room.

Hunkered on top of the steam table, I watched this tableau shuffle off to my left, and then I looked to my right, toward the ballroom end of the corridor, and my heart broke.

There, on his back, his shirt torn wide, his mouth open, his eyes rolling back in his head, his bloodied right hand clutching a rosary, his right ear a red smear, a blood-soaked handkerchief on his bare stomach, lay Bob Kennedy.

Behind him on the gray concrete floor was Paul Schrade, a Los Angeles official of the United Auto Workers Union, who appeared gravely, even mortally, injured. But Schrade recovered after surgery from a head wound and a fractured skull. Four others were shot. They lay about or limped about in the background, shocked and disbelieving that events had reached out to cut them down—Elizabeth Evans of Saugus, California, hit at the hairline by a bullet that embedded in her skull but did not penetrate it; nineteen-year-old Ira Goldstein of Continental News Service at Sherman Oaks, California, struck in the left thigh; Irwin Stroll, seventeen, of Los Angeles, wounded in the left shin, and William Weisel, the thirty-year-old associate director of the Washington bureau of ABC News, shot in the left side near the abdomen.

I jumped from the steam table and went to Ethel and Bob. She appeared calm as she knelt over her fallen husband, a tiger protecting her cub. She cooed to him. His jaw worked as if he were talking, or trying to. She looked up quickly when I dropped to one knee beside her, and I saw that her eyes were wide and excited, although her voice and her movements were deliberate and controlled.

"Help me," she said.

I mumbled that an ambulance and a doctor were on the way.

A uniformed hotel guard dashed in among the thirty or so people still milling aimlessly in the little kitchen corridor. His eyes were glinting and he was breathing in gulps. He pulled a revolver from its holster and looked around wildly.

"Put that thing away," Bill Barry said softly. And the guard did, and he withdrew. Bill looked at me, his blue Irish eyes in anguish.

"Help me get these people out of here, please," he said.

To a campaign aide huddled in a corner, crying and clutching Bob's shoes, Barry said:

"Stop crying and do your job. Get these people out. Clear an aisle for the ambulance people."

Barry and I began circling the room, pushing people out at both ends. Ethel stopped another hotel guard who started to lift Bob from the floor for some inexplicable reason.

"Wait!" she cried. "Don't raise his head! Get a doctor!"

A man took off his jacket and began fanning Bob with it.

"Get back, all of you!" Ethel begged. "Get out! Please, get out! For God's sake, give him room to breathe!"

Upstairs in the Kennedy's suite, a young boy sat transfixed in front of a television set, watching the milling crowds in the ballroom below and trying to comprehend what was happening to his father and mother. David Kennedy, who would be thirteen in less than two weeks, was all alone. His little brothers and sisters were already asleep. He planned to wander downstairs shortly to see the party, but he figured a better place to watch his father's victory speech was where he was, in front of a big-screen TV. Somebody was supposed to come for him and take him downstairs. When it happened, though, nobody thought about him. He watched and his mouth fell open and he kept on watching, not crying or reacting in any way, just watching. He was all alone, until somebody happened in and saw him.

Downstairs, after more time had passed, two men in blue uniforms with Medical Attendant shoulder patches came through the main part of the kitchen, wheeling a wire-mesh hospital stretcher. By then, all but a few campaign staffers, reporters, photographers and family members had cleared out. All the while, Steve Smith had been on the microphone in the ballroom, softly calming people and coaxing them to leave the scene—one more superb piece of grace under pressure that night. Dick Tuck, a staffer who had jumped from the second floor window at the rear of the kitchen to lead the ambulance driver and the attendant up the elevator and past the shiny stainless steel equipment, joined me in helping put Bob on the wheeled stretcher.

"Gently, gently," Ethel said.

"Gently, gently," Barry echoed.

The ambulance men moved more quickly than gently. Bob grimaced and rolled his head from side to side, and I saw the ugly little hole in the mastoid area just behind the right ear. I knew then that he would die, or that, if he survived through some medical miracle or lucky chance, he would never again be the man we knew.

"Oh, no! Don't!" Bob cried as he was moved. And those were the last words I heard him speak, ever. He fell completely unconscious.

One of the medical attendants, tugging on a kind of leash, whipped the stretcher around so that Bob's head was at the front as they started off at a trot through the main part of the kitchen toward the elevator at its rear. The stretcher banged into one piece of kitchen equipment, caromed off it and struck another. Barry was pleading, "Gently, gently!" But the attendants paid him no mind.

In the little service elevator, the attendant began, in a loud voice, giving instructions as to how he and the driver would get Bob to a hospital. He sounded incredibly officious, like a drill sergeant laying down the law to a new batch of recruits.

"Please lower your voice," Ethel said.

But he kept right on with his instructions as to who could ride in the ambulance and who could not—on and on and on. Blanche Whittaker, wife of the mountain climber, said, "Oh!" and reached out a white-gloved hand that half-swatted, half-brushed the attendant's mouth.

"Don't do that again, lady, or somebody will get a crushed head!" the man growled.

Before anybody could say or do more, the elevator landed and its wooden door flew up. There was a loading ramp, and the stretcher started down it at a breakneck speed.

"Gently, gently . . . somebody grab that thing!" Bill Barry called out. I was the closest. I reached out and grasped the rear of the device, slowing it.

"Let go!" the attendant shouted. But I held on until we cleared the ramp and reached the rear of the waiting ambulance.

By then, we had lost Blanche Whittaker and Bob's sister, Jean Smith, who had also been in the elevator. Bob and the stretcher were loaded aboard the ambulance and Ethel was helped in alongside him.

"Only Mrs. Kennedy rides with him," the attendant declared, starting to close the door. But Fred Dutton pushed him aside without a word and got in. As the doors started to close again, Bill Barry sought to enter, saying, "I belong in there." The attendant blocked his way. Barry drew back an arm and I grabbed it.

"Get in the front, Bill," I said, and he followed me. I helped him in and, without thinking why, jumped in beside him and slammed the door. The driver got in on the other side and started the ambulance engine.

But we could go nowhere. A Los Angeles Police Department patrol car was directly in front of us, making it impossible to move until it moved, and there was no driver inside. Dick Tuck, ever quick-thinking and fast-acting, got behind the wheel of the police car and tried to get it started. Failing, he released the brakes and began to push it.

"Hey, hey, what the hell are you doing?" a policeman yelled, grabbing Tuck and spinning him around. Tuck talked fast, and the officer hopped in, started the car and took off, a lead escort, red light flashing and siren wailing, to Central Receiving Hospital, a few short blocks away. We followed along.

In the ambulance, Barry pleaded with the driver for a smooth ride. We craned our necks to look back through a small window at the rear of the cab opening onto the vehicle's rear.

Bob's feet were toward us. Ethel and Dutton were bent over him at his left side. The attendant was on his right. Ethel looked up and our eyes met. I tried, by some process of will on my part, by some silent telegraphy of looking hard and earnestly at her, to reassure her that, somehow, everything would be all right. Her eyes were even more frantic now, and she made a kind of choking motion with one hand, running it quickly up and down her throat. Her lips seemed to be saying, "He can't breathe!"

Dutton and I both yelled at the same time, "He can't breathe . . . Oxygen . . . Oxygen!"

The attendant, who now seemed to move with excruciatingly slow deliberation, reached over and produced a plastic oxygen mask. As we watched in horror, he roughly stretched the elastic band attached to it over Bob's head, scraping across the bullet wound that gaped behind his right ear.

Ethel's eyes widened, her mouth gaped, and she shivered all over, as if seized with a chill.

At the hospital, we were out of the ambulance, up a ramp and loping down a corridor in a flash. As we rounded a corner, a lone photographer lay in wait. He made a picture quickly and backed up a step, starting to shoot again. Ethel let out a little cry and threw herself at him, lowering her right shoulder and making a perfect brush block as we wheeled on by.

"No picture!" Dutton cried, for no reason that he can think of to this day, and he pounced on the camera dangling from the poor man's neck. Barry grabbed him around the head from behind, and all three went skittering down the hall.

Deep inside the emergency area, we wheeled Bob into a room that had glass walls on three sides. It was small, and Dutton, Barry and I stepped outside it, leaving Ethel with her husband and six or eight doctors and nurses. We stood just outside, looking in through the huge glass panels.

One doctor, Dr. V. Faustin Bazilauskas, examined Bob quickly and slapped his face, calling out his name as he did. "Bob!" *Slap!* "Bob!" *Slap!* "Bob!"

Another member of the team, Dr. Albert Holt, jumped up on a stool and began an emergency heart massage, pressing fiercely against Bob's naked chest in a steady rhythm.

At first there was no heartbeat and no breathing detectable. Gradually, as the doctors worked, both came back. Ethel listened through Dr. Bazilauskas's stethoscope and nodded, almost smiling.

Outside the glassed-in room, Father James Mundell, a Maryknoll priest who was a friend of the Kennedy family, finally caught up with us. Ethel had tried to get him into the ambulance at the hotel. When the attendant kept him out, she signaled to him to follow us to the hospital. He had made it, but he looked very un-priestlike in a navy blue blazer, gray slacks and pale blue oxford button-down shirt, open at the collar, with no necktie, and the uniformed guard refused to let him go to Bob. Ethel saw the commotion and came out.

Just then, the guard gave Father Mundell a forearm blow across the chest and he reeled backward. Ethel grabbed the guard, and he spun around and hit Ethel in the chest with a forearm. Dutton jumped in and demanded the priest's admittance.

The guard relented, and Father Mundell gave Bob absolution of all his sins. Soon afterward, a priest from Los Angeles's St. Basil Church, Father Thomas Peacha, arrived and administered Extreme Unction, the last rites of the Roman Catholic Church, sprinkling Bob with holy water and anointing him with holy oil.

Others were arriving: Steve Smith, Adam Walinsky, Theodore Sorensen, Richard Goodwin, Pierre Salinger. The guards admitted them as campaign aides, but they kept hordes of reporters at bay outside the hospital's emergency entrance. Salinger came directly up the corridor to me walking quickly.

"How is he?" he asked.

I looked at him but said nothing.

"Where is he hit?" he asked.

"In the head," I said.

Pierre sagged. "Oh, no!" he cried, his voice twisted in anguish. I could almost feel him thinking, "Not again!" President Kennedy, for whom Pierre had been White House press secretary, had been shot in the head too.

Pierre put his head on my shoulder, like a child, and sobbed, once. I embraced him and patted him, like a comforting parent. We stood like that for a brief moment, this tough man and I who had had so many harsh words in our sometimes hectic reporter-advocate confrontations.

And then Pierre stiffened, lifted his head, and quickly walked away. He had been through it before.

Dun Gifford, another campaign staffer, who had been part of the crowd in the kitchen struggling to get the assailant's pistol, came up to me with a doleful expression on his face.

"Warren, you're the only reporter in here," he said, quietly, "and the guys outside have spotted you and they want to know why they can't be here too, and it would make things a lot easier if you would . . . "

I interrupted, "Sure, Dun, I'll leave."

And I did, stopping to tell the reporters outside all I knew about what had transpired. As we were talking, Bob was wheeled out a side entrance. Oxygen tubes extended from both nostrils. Other tubes into his arms provided plasma and dextrose. Ethel walked alongside, at Bob's head, and entered the rear of the ambulance. Bill Barry and David Hackett, one of Bob's closest friends and aides, who had been with him since prep school, took the front seat along with the driver. It was only a few blocks to Good Samaritan Hospital, where Bob was taken to a fifth-floor intensive care unit and then to surgery on the ninth floor.

Bob had been shot shortly after midnight, but it was not until 3:12 in the morning that the operation actually began. It lasted three hours and forty minutes, and it was conducted by a team of three neurosurgeons and three chest surgeons from the medical units of the University of Southern California and the University of California, Los Angeles. In charge was Dr. Maxwell M. Ander, a UCLA neurosurgeon. Assisting him were Dr. Henry Cuneo and Dr. Nat Downes Reid, also neurosurgeons, and Dr. Hubert Humble, Dr. Paul Ironside and Dr. Burt Meyer, all chest surgeons.

Dr. James Poppen of the Lahey Clinic in Boston, where Senator Edward M. Kennedy, Bob's younger brother, had been brought back to health after a 1964 airplane crash broke his back, was flown in (aboard an aircraft made available by Vice

President Hubert H. Humphrey). But he arrived after the operation was over.

The surgeons found three wounds. One bullet had grazed his forehead and another had lodged in the back of his neck. The third had entered the mastoid bone, shattering it into countless fragments that pierced the brain, and came to rest in the midline of the brain. The first two wounds were superficial. But the third one confirmed what we who had seen it back in the hotel kitchen had feared. There was almost no hope.

Outside the hospital, *LOOK* photographer Stan Tretick and I set up our vigil along with other photographers and reporters. We checked out of the Ambassador and moved into a modest little hotel around the corner from the hospital. We wandered around the police barricades and into a physicians' parking lot, where television crews had deployed their mobile units spewing out miles of cables spaghettied around the lot's asphalt surface, and somebody had even created a kind of press conference area, where Bob's press secretary, Frank Mankiewicz, appeared from time to time with medical bulletins.

At one point, Charles Evers, the civil rights leader, came to me in the parking lot. We had known each other since segregationists had murdered his brother, Medgar Evers, then head of the Mississippi unit of the National Association for the Advancement of Colored People. I had covered the funeral in Jackson and marched in the funeral procession with Charles, comedian Dick Gregory, Clarence Mitchell of the NAACP's Washington office, Dr. Martin Luther King, Jr., and others.

"Is he going to make it?" Evers asked, his face contorted.

"I don't think so," I said.

"Oh, no!" he cried. "God wouldn't do that to us! We can't lose him now!"

And once more I found myself comforting a strong man as he sobbed on my shoulder.

20

Ethel Alone

The 1968 California presidential primary was on Tuesday, June 4, and Sirhan Sirhan shot Robert Kennedy that night about ten minutes past midnight, California time. He died about twenty-four hours later, on June 6. He was waked at Saint Patrick's Cathedral in New York City, his body lying in state as thousands shuffled past his casket, and taken by funeral train on Saturday, June 8, to Washington, where he was buried at dusk, by the light of hundreds of hand-held candles, in Arlington National Cemetery next to his brother John. At the small, simple, almost insignificant grave site later, a small child was heard to ask his father who he was, and the father replied, "He was Attorney General and a Senator and he died."

It was bright and sunny that day at Hickory Hill with temperatures in the eighties. Workmen buzzed around mowing the grass, snipping the hedges and scrubbing the pool. Inside the big grayish-white house, servants cleaned and cooked as if it were just another idyllic day in the happiest of households. But soon, as the horrifying word came, every television set in the house was on and the radios too, and, even as they performed their normal routines, the people puttering about might have realized that nothing would be normal again.

The only Kennedy at Hickory Hill that day was the baby, Douglas. Tending him was the estimable Ena Bernard, the nanny who had helped rear all ten of the children and whom Bob Kennedy called "our treasure." At fourteen months, Dougie was too little to make the trip with Ethel to California. She had six children with her—David, Courtney, Michael, Kerry, Christopher and Max. The three oldest ones—Kathleen, Joe and Bobby—were away at school.

By the afternoon, Hickory Hill was bustling with travel preparations. In charge was Ethel's close friend from Manhattanville days, Katherine Evans, the wife of journalist Rowland Evans. Ethel had called her pal Kaysie with a request that she make sure the children got to New York City. Kathleen, Joe, Bobby and the baby were due at the Kennedy apartment at United Nations Plaza. Services, she was told, would be at Saint Patrick's Cathedral in New York City. Bob would be buried beside his brother Jack at Arlington National Cemetery in Washington.

Even as Ethel approved these plans and relayed them to family and friends, a change was coming over her. She had been Bob Kennedy's wholehearted helpmate, blind in her loyalty and helpless in her dependence. He had sheltered her, even against her own rash impulses—"Eth-el-l, don't say that. . . . Down, girl!" Now he was gone. She would have to make her own way, acting and deciding without him, but drawing on his memory to guide her—"What would Bobby do?"

And so she carried on, almost as if he were still there. Over the years, her celebrated temper would mellow and servants no longer would go in and out of Hickory Hill as if through a revolving door. But, then, the social pace there slowed as time passed and the children grew up and went off to lives of their own. Fewer and fewer servants found it an easier and easier place to work as the pace slowed. There was far less to be frenetic about.

Ethel's attention shifted from children to grandchildren in the normal course of time. The various organizations created to carry on Bob's work became thriving institutions. She maintained an active role in health foundations, like those for cancer research and aid to mentally retarded children, and in the Robert F. Kennedy Memorials honoring journalists, authors and social activists who labor on behalf of the poor and downtrodden.

For her, there never was much chance of a second marriage. She once said, "Marry again? With Bobby looking down from Heaven? That would be *adultery*." It was meant as a joke, but her friends would not dispute the basic truth of it. From the time of Bob's death, she fully expected to meet him again in the hereafter, and she could never face him then with a conscience stained by the infidelity of having married someone else.

She could even joke about that:

"All the men who are interesting are all married or used to be married. You know what's going to happen? When I get to be eighty-five, the Vatican is going to say it's okay to marry a divorced man. What's more, it's going to say, it's *always* been okay."

Nevertheless, she was wounded by the rumor mills and the lurid journalism found at checkout counters and on syndicated television. First, there was gossip about Bob and his sister-in-law Jacqueline soon after President Kennedy's assassination, when they spent much time together consoling each other. And then, after Bob's death, came a flood of speculation about an affair with movie queen Marilyn Monroe, fed by the public's growing fascination with the private lives of public figures.

Angela Novello, who was Bob's secretary for many years, scoffed at the stories about Marilyn Monroe. She talked by telephone regularly with her and she was "drawn to her sweetness and vulnerability," Angie said. She went on:

"She called often to chat, to hear a sympathetic voice. If Bob was not in, I would talk with her, and she seemed just as pleased. That happened often. Ethel would talk to her at times, and, like me, she found her innocent and childlike.

"Sometimes Bob would call her back, sometimes not. Bob would listen, sympathize, cluck over something she said. He was a good listener, you know, a good shoulder to cry on."

But, Angie was asked, what about his sense of adventure? He climbed mountains and ran rapids, always drawn to danger, testing himself. Could he have been tempted to see what it would be like to consort with the Love Goddess?

"Perhaps. But that would have been totally out of character," Angie said. "As genuinely devout as he was, and as devoted to Ethel and his family, I don't see how he would have risked all that—and Heaven too, which he believed in—for a fling? It's doubtful. It's out of character."

There was one other thing, Angie said:

"The day after Marilyn's death, when I went to the office, we talked about it. Bob shook his head and agreed with me that it was a shame Marilyn had died so young and so unhappy. And then he started giving orders and we got to work.

"Now, I know Bob Kennedy, and I know that, if there had been any special bond between him and Marilyn, he would have been in tears or close to it, right after her death. He cried when his brother died. Oh, how he suffered! He fell into a depression that I thought he would never come out of. He was always that way when he was dealt a blow or faced problems. He would sit and stare. His hands would tremble. It would be hard to get his attention.

"But, with Marilyn's passing, he reacted as he would to the death of anyone he might have known but not known well. He couldn't fake a thing like that. I would have known."

That would be about the way Ethel would put it too, if she could ever come out from behind her pain and shyness. Meantime, she continued to do what she would do at Hickory Hill if

Bob were still with her—in retirement, perhaps, after two terms as President in the "Newer World" administration.

Friends speculated on what kind of a President Bob would have been, what kind of administration he would have run, what legacies he would have left, both good and troublesome. A few points can be made about these things on which most of those who knew Bob Kennedy would agree, it seems to me.

He liked the phrase "newer world" and probably would have applied it to his administration, in the tradition of Franklin Roosevelt's New Deal, Harry Truman's Fair Deal, Jack Kennedy's New Frontier and Lyndon Johnson's Great Society. He borrowed it from a passage in the works of Alfred, Lord Tennyson, that he often quoted and, in fact, used for the title of his 1967 book of essays, *To Seek a Newer World*. The passage:

> The lights begin to twinkle from the rocks:
> The long day wanes: the slow moon climbs: the deep
> Moans round with many voices. Come, my friends,
> 'Tis not too late to seek a newer world.
> Push off, and sitting well in order smite
> The sounding furrows; for my purpose holds
> To sail beyond the sunset, and the baths
> Of all the western stars, until I die.

If Sirhan's bullet had been an inch this way or that, Bob might have lived, unimpaired. He would then certainly have won the nomination and the election. As President, I am sure he would have kept Robert S. McNamara, whom he admired because "he got things done," in his cabinet, probably promoting him from Secretary of Defense to Secretary of State. A devoted and utterly responsible public servant like Cyrus R. Vance likely would have taken over McNamara's Pentagon post. Utilizing their skills and calling on others like them, such as Averell Harriman and Paul H. Nitze, a President Robert F. Kennedy would have ended the Vietnam War no later than

March of 1969. He would thereby have saved thirty-five thousand American lives—the total lost in the four years that the war dragged on under President Nixon and Secretary of State Henry M. Kissinger—and about a million Vietnamese lives. There would still be Americans in Vietnam though, as part of a President RFK's expanded Peace Corps, the project his brother launched and that he embraced as a significant and promising approach to Third World problems. Bob Kennedy probably would have turned Vietnam from bitter enemy to a showcase of American capitalism through full utilization of the Peace Corps's potential. He would have pursued his brother's call to negotiate without fear, not only with the Soviet Union, but also with Fidel Castro's Cuba. A presidential trip to Havana in search of a settlement would have had early priority. Similarly, there would have been openings to China and, especially, strong efforts for a Middle East settlement following the brief but disruptive Arab-Israeli War of 1967.

On the home front, a President RFK would have pushed VISTA, the domestic counterpart of the Peace Corps. He would have put somebody like John Doar, a trusted aide at the Justice Department in civil rights disturbances, in charge of VISTA with instructions to wipe out slums like Watts in Los Angeles and Bedford-Stuyvesant in New York City. He would want them too to become showcases of American capitalism. Similarly vigorous efforts would have been aimed at the rural slums of Appalachia and elsewhere. He would have drawn closer to the nation's campuses, scenes of so much unrest in the sixties, with people like Sam Brown and John Kerry and other young activists as liaisons and advisers. As President, Bob Kennedy would still have had trouble winning support from the South, which was continuing to oppose civil rights reforms, and from what former Census Bureau Director Richard Scammon calls the "nonblack, nonpoor, nonyoung" of salaried suburbia.

Academicians would have been welcomed enthusiastically into the RFK administration, just as they had been brought to

Hickory Hill for long evenings of brainstorming at the Hickory Hill Academy. A President who admitted he was only a fair student and came to books late would have pushed education for the nation, just as he pushed it for his children around the dining room table at Hickory Hill. So too with employing women and minorities in his administration. Women like Gloria Steinem and Marian Edelman would certainly have had significant appointments, and it is entirely possible that Charles E. Smith, a black lawyer from Seattle who worked for Bob at the Justice Department, would have become the second black jurist on the Supreme Court alongside the first, Thurgood Marshall. In all likelihood, J. Edgar Hoover would have been removed as director of the Federal Bureau of Investigation, with his successor, possibly Ramsey Clark, ordered to launch an all-out effort against organized crime and its accursed offspring, the traffic in illegal drugs.

In short, a President Robert Kennedy would have sought to do the things he was promising to do when he was cut down, for he was that rarity among politicians and, for that matter, among humans: he meant what he said, and he kept his promises. He would have worked for a renewal of national self-confidence based on more substance than chants of "U - S - A!" and televised rocketry.

Even more important than what might have been is what might *not* have been. If Sirhan's bullet had indeed struck Bob Kennedy's mastoid bone an inch higher or lower, or an inch to the left or the right, he might have survived without impairment and gone on, perhaps helped by a sympathy vote, to the nomination and the election. Ending the Vietnam War in 1969, as he promised, would have done even more than save the lives of thirty-five thousand Americans, plus all the children they would never have. There would have been no more of the divisive bitterness that plagued the Nixon administration and, with no Richard M. Nixon in the White House, there would have been no Watergate scandal and nothing to put in the history books about a President forced to resign.

*   *   *

Ethel Kennedy would never join in any such speculations and fantasizing. She found it fruitless and depressing and she had no time for self-pity. When friends sought to sympathize with what they saw as surely an aching loneliness, she would brush them off, sometimes not too gently, with, "How am I? What do I do with myself? I look after my kids, and I look after the Kennedy foundations. We stay busy here. There's not enough time for everything."

Perfection was still the goal at Hickory Hill in the pursuit of excellence, whether in running a philanthropic foundation or chasing after a tennis ball. Ethel remains the keeper of the flame, in her own special way, and she is coping day by day, supporting her children and grandchildren as she supported Bob, until the time comes for her to rejoin him.

Epilogue

Fall was in the air, but there was still time for one more out-door gathering at Hickory Hill. Children ran recklessly around the swimming pool, most in wet swimsuits. They were every-where, and overwhelming. The smaller ones made the most racket, chasing each other in quick dashes, with sudden halts and dodges, followed by several dogs barking, yelping and snapping at their legs and ankles. The older children mostly lounged at poolside and in metal folding chairs inside the big pool house, where the soft drinks were. The bigger girls tugged at their bathing suits and glanced often toward the boys, who ignored them. A few of these were wrestling haphazardly, gang-ing up at times on one of their number to throw him into the pool, arms flailing and legs kicking. Their newly deepening voices honked in that raucous, unmelodious way peculiar to adolescent boys, a sound borrowed from geese and New Year's Eve horns, and they seemed never to tire of the noise, so new and beguiling to their ears.

Ethel Kennedy, tanned and freckled, sat in a plastic-roped lawn chair amid a small group of other women at the end of the pool away from the diving board. They were all smiling and chatting warmly, with a burst of laughter here and there as Ethel or Mary Douglas or Kay Evans or Liz Stevens or some other old friend said something funny. Other grown-ups were scattered about the poolside, and the men, outnumbered by wives and children, talked quietly in little bunches too. They swirled their glasses, the ice clinking, as if that would hurry along the beginning of the movie.

Chairs and sofas in catch-as-catch-can variety, whatever was available, were lined up in rows, theater-style, inside the pool house. A projectionist, hired for the night, already had set things up inside a booth built for that purpose at the rear. A large screen had been pulled down at the front of the room. All was in readiness. It was simply a question of when Ethel, or whoever else assumed command, would say, "Go!" And then the scramble would be on, to grab a seat and separate the smaller children from the pool and the dogs, calm down the dogs and the children, large and small, and settle into place for the start of the movie.

Up the steep grassy hill a hundred yards or so away, the house itself looked distant and detached and, at the same time, watchful and brooding. Hickory Hill had seen many such parties and other gatherings too, indoors and out. The big house always seemed distant and detached when scores, sometimes hundreds, of people gathered there to celebrate, mourn, or simply be together on a good outdoor kind of day.

I looked up the hill from poolside, conscious suddenly of how quickly the glare of that warm day was giving way to the soft light of early dusk. I felt acutely conscious then of the overwhelming bulk of the house on the hill, and of Bob's continuing presence there with Ethel at Hickory Hill. The squarish, white clapboard building, half hidden among towering trees and ancient bushes, seemed painfully of the past, an anachronism in proximity to the modern pool and all of its secure, laughing children, who, after all, were the future.

"Show time!" somebody yelled. "Everybody in for the movie!"

Some of the children rocketed into the pool house and began immediately fighting over places. Others entered under duress, dragged in by their mothers and protesting every step. Ethel wound up somewhere in the middle of the seating, claiming one of the more comfortable couches. I found myself in the very first row in a hard metal chair. I had not moved fast enough when the call sounded.

"What's the movie?" I asked a teenaged boy on my left.

"Beats me, sir," he replied. "Did you ask Mrs. Kennedy?"

"She doesn't know. Says it's some kind of a war movie."

I turned and surveyed the audience. Ethel was talking animatedly with somebody and, when she saw me looking, she waved good-naturedly and kept on talking. There was a yell from somewhere to turn off the lights. The lights went out and there was a burst of applause, followed by stomping, whistling and yelling. The cone of the projector light cut through the dark over our heads and flashed the Paramount logo on the screen. And then the title of the picture came up.

It was *Catch-22*.

I did not know much about *Catch-22*. I had read the book and, like most people, I suppose, had liked it despite feeling disturbed by its relentless, uncompromising, bitter hammering at war as full-blown idiocy. What little of the reviews of the movie I remembered had seemed to stress its more sensational aspects, like scenes of the war-worn airman climbing a tree in the nude. I wondered how we would cope with that, in this conglomeration of small children, adolescents, parents and perhaps—I looked around—a priest or a nun or two.

"I wish Ethel would have somebody screen these things ahead of time," I heard myself mumbling. It occurred to me that somebody might walk out on the film, if it was indeed as raw as I supposed it was. Self-conscious, I scrunched down in my chair.

It was worse than I had anticipated, but for another reason. There was a scene inside an American bomber in which a young man lay mortally wounded, eyes rolled back and glazed in shock, with a fellow crewman beside him trying frantically to keep him alive as their shot-up aircraft struggled toward its North African base. The stricken airman was on his back, his pressurized flight suit soaked with his blood. His arms and legs stuck out like a puppet's, useless and meaningless. The focal point was the face, ashen and spiritless, with those rolled-back blue eyes and the open mouth showing large white teeth.

When that scene ended, I realized I was sitting rigidly in the chair, straining every muscle. I stole a look back over my shoulder, and I saw that Ethel appeared to be in stress too, eyes wide and teeth clenched, remembering.

And then, to my horror, the same scene was back on the screen. Then it was gone, as the movie moved on to something else, and then it was back again, and it hit me that this scene of the dying young man would appear intermittently throughout most or all of the film, in repeated counterpoint to the main line of the action—on and on and on.

I looked back and saw Ethel's seat empty. I went outside and walked up the hill to the house. There were no stars. Darkness had not yet settled in completely. Off to the right, among some maple and oak trees, a terrible clatter arose: Caw! Caw! Caw! A half dozen or so crows were hopping and fluttering among the lower branches in a state of high agitation. Their behavior beguiled me as a mystery for a while, and then the cause appeared—a couple of blue jays, their voices like a witch's shriek, darted in and out, apparently deliberately trespassing on crow territory. The fight went on as I trudged up the hill, past the huge tree that hovers over the terrace at the rear of the house, and went inside.

Ethel was in a little room off the main entrance—the Kennedy children called it the TV room—connecting with the large living room that Bob and Ethel had added on as their family had continued to grow. She was sitting alone on the room's overstuffed sofa. The enormous television set that dominated the room stared blankly. She was simply sitting.

I dropped into a chair beside the sofa. Ethel tossed her head, as if to clear it of the bleak thoughts that were certainly there, and launched gaily into a chat about her children and some of the funny things that were said at poolside and whatever. She asked about my family, and we shared a story or two, going along like that until the people from the pool house, once the movie ended, began trooping into the house, looking for more drinks and more to eat. They came on like a summer shower, first the low murmur of voices up the hill, and then the louder scraping of feet on the terrace, and finally the full impact of everybody storming that much lived-in house, putting a sudden end to its calm.

A younger Kennedy, freckled and rabbit-toothed, came into the sitting room, seeking help on some special problem that could not wait. Ethel swooped him up in one practiced motion, saying, "Okay, okay, ol' Moms will fix." She pulled herself up from the too soft, too enveloping chintz sofa. I stood up also and stepped aside. Just before she left the room, she reached out and squeezed my hand.

"Thanks," she said, very quietly.

The stress, the half-wild look of panic that I had caught in her eyes earlier was gone. It would be back, I knew. But, for a while, it was laid to rest. I wondered how deeply she had suffered. It did not seem likely that she would ever tell anyone.

Bob Kennedy was forty-two years old when he died. He had been born into wealth that most people dare not dream about. Yet, he gave every ounce of his being, and eventually his life, to a personal fight against injustice and poverty, material and spiritual. He drove himself as if there were no end to his abilities and courage, and he made those around him wonder at times if that were not so. He experienced life to the full, and he grew with each experience, especially after the death of his brother John just five years before he himself was taken away.

I never hear *The Battle Hymn of the Republic*, a favorite of his, without thinking of him and of the courage of his widow. I remember how funny he was, and how he made us all laugh so much with his shy, little boy way of seeing things as they are, the grin, the earnestness and the haste.

That was the man we celebrated on that eight-hour train ride from New York to Washington. It was no funeral cortege but a gathering of friends of Bobby, and Ethel made sure that mood prevailed, coming through the cars with fifteen-year-old Joe at her side and the other children trailing behind, smiling greetings to every one of us.

And it was in his memory that those who reported the most on Bob's last campaign made sure we followed him to Arlington National Cemetery in a last campaign bus. Richard Drayne, a press aide and later press secretary to Senator Ted Kennedy, put a list together of those to be aboard, on the basis of who had been part of the traveling press in the eighty days of the campaign. He was guided by two reporters who had been along throughout, Richard Harwood of the *Washington Post* and Hays Gorey of *Time* magazine.

Drayne called ahead to the people in charge of the funeral to make sure they understood that the press bus was *sentimental* and *symbolic* and therefore had to be up near the front of the cavalcade from Washington's Union Station to Virginia's Arlington National Cemetery. It was not proper, he was told, to put a bus in a funeral motorcade. Remembering how Bob would have reacted, Drayne said, "Yeah, just do it."

At Union Station, Drayne found himself in a sea of black limousines. He asked where the special press bus was. When it was pointed out, he asked what position it would be in. He was told it would be twenty-third in line behind the hearse, and, without saying anything, he began to ponder how to change a situation that he found, in Bob's word, "unacceptable."

Campaign aide Dick Tuck was at the door of the bus with the list, admitting those named and rejecting all others. He turned away movie star Lauren Bacall, explaining she was not listed. He turned away Arthur M. Schlesinger, Jr., a key campaign adviser and later Bob's brilliant biographer, for the same reason. He turned away a United Press International reporter, who ranted and raved because his opposition, the Associated Press, was aboard. But Tuck held his ground: AP had had a reporter on the bus throughout the campaign and UPI had covered it with local people at each stop.

Drayne went up to him and said: "Tuck, I don't know why this bus ought to be twenty-three cars back. Do you?"

"No, I certainly do not," Tuck said.

To Frank Mankiewicz, the campaign press secretary, they said, "Frank, this bus is twenty-three cars back. Do you think . . . ?"

"No, it shouldn't be that far back," Frank said.

When the bus was loaded, they had the driver maneuver close to where the motorcade would be passing. Mankiewicz checked out each limousine as it went by, looking for family members. After a few had passed with no family aboard, somebody jumped out into the street and, holding up a hand with great authority, as they had done many times in many places in the campaign, halted the limousines. The bus moved in, about sixth in line.

As the procession rolled slowly through the heart of downtown Washington, it became obvious to us on the bus that limousines were trying to pass on both sides, as if embarrassed to be behind a press bus. The car in front of us stopped and what appeared to be a Secret Service agent with a hand radio climbed out and came toward us. Despite our yells, the driver opened the door and he got aboard.

Politely, almost apologetically, he began to explain that we had somehow blundered into the wrong place in line. He managed only a few words when the entire bus rose up yelling and screaming, "Get the hell off our bus!" Somebody charged at him, and he was physically pushed back through the door. Dick Tuck blew the shrill police whistle he used during the campaign to summon reporters to the bus. He never blew it harder, and it was for the last time.

"Okay, let's go," we said, and on we went.

But a tougher, smarter agent was waiting a few blocks on. He stood in the middle of the road, arms outstretched like a cormorant drying its wings, the pistol in his shoulder holster glinting in the streetlight. Our choices were to stop or to run him down. We stopped.

Mankiewicz and Tuck jumped out and began arguing with the fellow, who towered over them and kept saying, very quietly:

"You're not going anywhere."

Drayne took up a position about thirty feet in front of the bus, to block the limousines attempting to get by. He was daring them to run him over and, when one actually came at him with obvious intent, he reluctantly stepped aside.

Aboard the bus, we peered into the first limousine to pass. In the pale light, we saw the familiar face of President Lyndon B. Johnson. He was followed by six Secret Service cars and then a limousine bearing Vice President Hubert H. Humphrey.

They had, as Drayne observed later, "been breathing the exhaust of the press bus almost the entire way to the cemetery." Bob Kennedy would have loved it.

At Arlington, the world will remember a solemn burial ceremony, with thousands of hand-held candles twinkling like tiny stars in the dark of the cemetery's somber hills. From a distance, it must have looked like one more superb production by what many then called "the well-oiled Kennedy machine." But, up close, it was different. It was, in truth, a typical ad lib situation, half planned and hastily organized, that Bob always seemed to fall into and escape from in triumph.

The pallbearers were told only to walk up a hill, bear left and stop. In the dark, uncertain of their footing, trying to maintain a dignified pace, they kept walking and looking for where they were supposed to be. Stephen Smith, Bob's campaign manager and husband of his sister Jean, was searching for a place to stop, as the lead pallbearer, without betraying his dilemma.

Pallbearer Averell Harriman said, "Steve, do you know where you're going?"

"Well, I'm not sure," Smith said.

Pallbearer John Seigenthaler, an aide to Bob and later editor of the Nashville *Tennessean*, said, "I have a feeling we've walked too far."

"So do I," Smith said. "Let's stop, and you go over and ask the man where we should be."

"No, *you* go," Seigenthaler said. "You're the campaign manager."

Smith asked the first person who looked as if he might know something, and the man said, "You've been doing fine, but you've just gone a little too far."

Seigenthaler started laughing, and so did some of the others. He said later, "I could hear Bobby laughing and saying, 'You *really* screwed it up—again!'"

Smith said later, "I distinctly heard a voice coming out of the coffin saying, 'Damn it, put me down and I'll show you the way.'"

His mother remembered that Bob, as the seventh of her nine children, was overshadowed by his older brothers, who were bigger and stronger and "brilliant" in school. He "had to work extra hard to make his record equal theirs," Rose Kennedy wrote, for a set of remembrances assembled by her daughter Patricia, the sister whom Bob loved to call "Beauty." She went on:

"Bobby had a consuming passion to do what he thought was right and the will and the vigor to pursue that goal regardless of physical fatigue or difficulties. . . . He accepted life's challenges and . . . rejoiced in life's gifts and laughed and sang and played too, with zest and enthusiasm. He was a deeply religious man, a fact for which his father and I were very grateful.

"How sad are our hearts when we realize that we shall never see Bobby again, with his tousled, windblown hair, his big, affectionate smile, carrying one child piggyback and holding another by the hand—his dog close behind. What joy he brought us. What an aching void he has left behind, which nothing in the world can ever fill. We admired him, we loved him, and our lives are indeed bleak without him. . . .

"I know that I shall not look upon his like again."

Bob was technically Jack Kennedy's little brother, but he watched over him like a big brother, almost from the first day he walked into Kennedy campaign headquarters in Boston reporting to Dave Powers for assignment. It was 1946, he was twenty years old, just coming out of the Navy and returning to Harvard and, even then, as Powers recalled, he "wanted to work where it would do the most good." He was in fact Ted Kennedy's big brother and watched over him all his life. In Ted's way of thinking, Bob is watching over the whole Kennedy clan. He wrote in memoriam:

When I think of Bobby, I shall always see Cape Cod on a sunny day. The wind will be from the southwest and the white caps will be showing and the full tide will be sweeping through the gaps in the breakwater. It will be after lunch, and Bob will be stripped to the waist and he'll say:

"Come on, Joe! Kathleen! Bobby and David! Courtney! Kerry! Come on, Michael, and even you, Chris and Max! Call your mother and come on for a sail!"

One of the children will say, "What about the baby?"

And the father will say, "Douglas can come next year."

They push off from the landing. The sails of the *Resolute* catch the wind, and the boat tips and there are squeals of laughter from the crew.

And Bob says, "I think today is the day we'll tip over!"

And there are more squeals and the *Resolute* reaches toward the end of the breakwater with a bubbling wake left behind. Beyond the breakwater, its bow rises and falls with the rhythm of the sea, the children are covered with spray, and he will dive overboard and catch hold of the line that trails behind, inviting the children to join him. Child after child jumps into the water, grabbing for the line, and those who appear to miss it are pulled toward it by his strong and suntanned arms.

The boat heads out into Nantucket Sound. The tide is gentle, the sand shifts, the sky is blue, the seagulls watch from above and the breeze is warm. And there will be happiness and love and we are together again.

While managing the 1960 campaign that won the presidency for his brother, Bob turned one day to his cousin, Polly Fitzgerald, a campaign stalwart from the beginning, and asked:

"If you had a choice of dying and going straight to Heaven, or of living and taking your chances, which would you choose?"

Polly replied that she would live and take her chances.

"Not me," Bob said. "I'd take the other."

Eight years later, poised but hesitant about running for the White House himself, he had virtually the same conversation with Polly and with the same results.

"He told me he would still make the same choice," she said. "It comforts me now to know this and to remember his simple faith in God's promises."

He was forty-two when he died, and I knew him only for the last twelve. John Douglas's casual aside to me one day, so profound, still haunts me. Douglas, son of Illinois's great Senator Paul Douglas, and a campaign aide and family friend, said:

"Who really knew Bob Kennedy?"

Who, indeed, among all who try to explain him.

There was much, much, much that he showed to nobody.

Except Ethel, perhaps. And sometimes their children. And very, very few others.

Index